Advance praise for **Profits You Can Trust —**

"This book blasts through misleading financials."

Bruce Wasserstein
Head of Lazard

"Tired of getting snookered on financial accounting issues in your investments? Worried about your ability to exercise adequate financial oversight as a board member? This concise, readable, authoritative book will enable you to spot accounting landmines without earning a CPA. A must-read for all investors and overseers!"

Regina E. Herzlinger
Nancy R. McPherson Professor of Business
Administration Chair, Harvard Business School
Current and former director of 12 publicly traded corporations
A "financial expert" under the current SEC definition

"This comprehensive layman's guide is a must-read for senior management, boards, committees, and their advisors. Writing in largely non-technical language, the expert authors provide the most concise and complete road map to understanding, preventing, detecting, and remediating accounting and reporting shenanigans that I have read."

C. Russel Hansen, Jr.
Former President and CEO, National Association
    of Corporate Directors
Former Senior Partner, Hale & Dorr
Founder and Managing Director of The Board Place.

"This enjoyable book has valuable insights for board members, analysts, and stock and bond managers. In my three-plus decades of managing money, this is one of the most user-friendly, as well as expert, books I have seen on this subject. We can all make great use of it."

Fred Kobrick
Former manager of the State Street Capital Fund
One of *USA Today*'s Top 5 funds of the 15-year bull market

"If shady accounting is detectable to outsiders, *Profits You Can Trust* will show you how to spot it. A must read for every investor who wants to avoid or profit from questionable corporate accounting."

David Hawkins
Lovett-Learned Professor of Business Administration,
Harvard Business School

"This book performs an extremely valuable service for investors by explaining in clear terms the variations on basic tricks that manipulate the figures in business. It will help investors spot red flags early, and belongs on every investor's book shelf."

Dr. Cynthia J. Smith
Ohio State University, and co-author of *Inside Arthur Andersen*

PROFITS
you can
TRUST

FT Prentice Hall

FINANCIAL TIMES

In an increasingly competitive world, it is quality
of thinking that gives an edge, an idea that opens new
doors, a technique that solves a problem, or an insight
that simply helps make sense of it all.

We work with leading authors in the various arenas
of business and finance to bring cutting-edge thinking
and best learning practice to a global market.

It is our goal to create world-class print publications
and electronic products that give readers
knowledge and understanding they can
apply while studying or at work.

To find out more about our business
products, you can visit us at www.ft-ph.com

Pearson
Education

H. David Sherman • S. David Young • Harris Collingwood

PROFITS
you can
TRUST

Spotting & Surviving
Accounting Landmines

FT Prentice Hall
FINANCIAL TIMES

An Imprint of PEARSON EDUCATION
Upper Saddle River, NJ • New York • San Francisco • Toronto • Sydney
Tokyo • Singapore • Hong Kong • Cape Town • Madrid
Paris • Milan • Munich • Amsterdam

www.ft-ph.com

Library of Congress Cataloging-in-Publication Data

A CIP catalog record for this book can be obtained from the Library of Congress

Editorial/Production Supervision: Wil Mara
Cover Design Director: Jerry Votta
Cover Design: Nina Scuderi
Art Director: Gail Cocker-Bogusz
Manufacturing Manager: Alexis R. Heydt-Long
Executive Editor: Jim Boyd
Editorial Assistant: Linda Ramagnano
Marketing Manager: John Pierce

© 2003 Pearson Education, Inc.
Publishing as Financial Times Prentice Hall
Upper Saddle River, New Jersey 07458

Prentice Hall PTR offers excellent discounts on this book when ordered in quantity for bulk purchases or special sales. For more information, please contact: U.S. Corporate and Government Sales, 1-800-382-3419, corpsales@pearsontechgroup.com. For sales outside of the U.S., please contact: International Sales, 1-317-581-3793, or via the Web at international@pearsontechgroup.com.

Printed in the United States of America

First Printing

ISBN 0-13-100196-5

Pearson Education Ltd.
Pearson Education Australia Pty., Limited
Pearson Education Singapore, Pte. Ltd.
Pearson Education North Asia Ltd.
Pearson Education Canada, Ltd.
Pearson Educación de Mexico, S.A. de C.V.
Pearson Education—Japan
Pearson Education Malaysia, Pte. Ltd.

DEDICATIONS

"To Linda, Amanda, and Caroline."

—HDS

"To Katherine Blanco."

—HC

FINANCIAL TIMES PRENTICE HALL BOOKS

For more information, please go to www.ft-ph.com

Business and Technology

Sarv Devaraj and Rajiv Kohli

> *The IT Payoff: Measuring the Business Value of Information Technology Investments*

Nicholas D. Evans

> *Business Innovation and Disruptive Technology: Harnessing the Power of Breakthrough Technology…for Competitive Advantage*

Nicholas D. Evans

> *Consumer Gadgets: 50 Ways to Have Fun and Simplify Your Life with Today's Technology…and Tomorrow's*

Faisal Hoque

> *The Alignment Effect: How to Get Real Business Value Out of Technology*

Economics

David Dranove

> *What's Your Life Worth? Health Care Rationing…Who Lives? Who Dies? Who Decides?*

John C. Edmunds

> *Brave New Wealthy World: Winning the Struggle for World Prosperity*

Jonathan Wight

> *Saving Adam Smith: A Tale of Wealth, Transformation, and Virtue*

Entrepreneurship

Oren Fuerst and Uri Geiger

> *From Concept to Wall Street: A Complete Guide to Entrepreneurship and Venture Capital*

David Gladstone and Laura Gladstone

> *Venture Capital Handbook: An Entrepreneur's Guide to Raising Venture Capital, Revised and Updated*

Erica Orloff and Kathy Levinson, Ph.D.

> *The 60-Second Commute: A Guide to Your 24/7 Home Office Life*

Jeff Saperstein and Daniel Rouach

> *Creating Regional Wealth in the Innovation Economy: Models, Perspectives, and Best Practices*

Finance

Aswath Damodaran
The Dark Side of Valuation: Valuing Old Tech, New Tech, and New Economy Companies

Kenneth R. Ferris and Barbara S. Pécherot Petitt
Valuation: Avoiding the Winner's Curse

International Business

Peter Marber
Money Changes Everything: How Global Prosperity Is Reshaping Our Needs, Values, and Lifestyles

Fernando Robles, Françoise Simon, and Jerry Haar
Winning Strategies for the New Latin Markets

Investments

Zvi Bodie and Michael J. Clowes
Worry-Free Investing: A Safe Approach to Achieving Your Lifetime Goals

Harry Domash
Fire Your Stock Analyst! Analyzing Stocks on Your Own

David Gladstone and Laura Gladstone
Venture Capital Investing: The Complete Handbook for Investing in New Businesses, New and Revised Edition

D. Quinn Mills
Buy, Lie, and Sell High: How Investors Lost Out on Enron and the Internet Bubble

D. Quinn Mills
Wheel, Deal, and Steal: Deceptive Accounting, Deceitful CEOs, and Ineffective Reforms

John Nofsinger and Kenneth Kim
Infectious Greed: Restoring Confidence in America's Companies

John R. Nofsinger
Investment Blunders (of the Rich and Famous)...And What You Can Learn from Them

John R. Nofsinger
Investment Madness: How Psychology Affects Your Investing...And What to Do About It

H. David Sherman, S. David Young, and Harris Collingwood
Profits You Can Trust: Spotting & Surviving Accounting Landmines

Leadership

Jim Despain and Jane Bodman Converse
And Dignity for All: Unlocking Greatness through Values-Based Leadership

TABLE OF CONTENTS

PREFACE

When work began in earnest on this book in the fall of 2002, the Enron scandal was barely a year old. Harvey Pitt was still chairman of the Securities and Exchange Commission and was still advocating that regulators adopt a "kinder, gentler" attitude toward the corporations under their purview. As this preface is being written in late May of 2003, it is hard to know just how much has changed. Pitt is gone, replaced by William H. Donaldson; Congress has passed the Sarbanes-Oxley Act, which imposes broad new financial disclosure obligations on publicly held corporations and their officers; and the Securities and Exchange Commission is formulating new rules requiring corporate boards to certify the steps they are taking to combat fraud.

The very fact that the SEC is drawing up those rules suggests that where corporate accounting and accountability are concerned, little has fundamentally changed. The business news this spring is full of fresh scandal: The Netherlands-based Ahold Corporation admits that even after restating $880 million in earnings, it cannot say for sure that it has identified all the accounting irregularities on the books of its U.S. operations. The CEO of Tenet Healthcare resigns, his tenure tainted by the misleading disclosures that occurred on his watch. And the president of the New York Stock Exchange, Richard Grasso, has his hands full: brokers on the floor of the NYSE are alleged to have systematically cheated investors, and corporate-governance watchdogs are howling at Grasso's multimillion-dollar pay package.

In the face of such evidence, it seems safe to conclude that corporate arrogance and executive-suite cluelessness have survived the stock market collapse and the endless scandals that have followed. Reason enough, then, for a guide to the many varieties of deceptive corporate accounting. Who needs this guide? When we began work on the article that was the foundation for the present book, our intended audience consisted of corporate directors and officers, then facing a new mandate to demonstrate "financial literacy." But it quickly became clear to us that if corporate board members needed to be financially literate, then so did those to whom those board members were ultimately answerable: investors, securities analysts, journalists, and the public at large. The present volume, then, is intended both for corporate insiders and for corporate outsiders. Both have a stake in honest, transparent corporate financial disclosure.

Although this book is concerned with the use and misuse of accounting techniques, it does not require expert knowledge of the subject. It presumes only a rudimentary acquaintance with accounting practices and terminology. Far more important than technical knowledge, as we point out throughout the book, is a skeptical, inquiring attitude. That attitude might well have prevented many of accounting disasters we discuss in this book. The sources for the stories we recount in these pages include contemporaneous press accounts, public documents, and our own experiences in business, higher education, and journalism. We hope that by examining past cases of untrustworthy corporate accounting, we can help readers identify future cases – before they turn into disaster stories. And we hope that by encouraging the practice of informed skepticism, we contribute to a business environment where profits—and the corporations that report them—are again worthy of our trust.

As we present this book to the public, David Sherman (h.sherman@neu.edu) wishes to make the following acknowledgements:

I am indebted to three colleagues and friends at Northeastern University who made this book possible by enabling me to embark on a research sabbatical at INSEAD, in Fontainebleau, France. Professor Paul Janell, the chair of the accounting group, has continually allowed me to pursue exciting new intellectual challenges. Words cannot adequately capture the thanks I owe to Paul. When I told Senior Associate Dean Jim Molloy that I had been invited to INSEAD, his immediate response was, "You've got to do it and take your whole family." The wisdom of Jim's encouragement continues to astound me. Ira Weiss, Dean of Northeastern and facilitator of all manner of remarkable ideas, provided a chaired professorship that added valuable momentum to the process. These three colleagues gave me a chance to observe the business world from Paris, where the activities of North America, Asia and Europe are reported with equal weight. The perspective gained in those days before the Enron debacle reinforced my conviction that accounting games were ubiquitous and becoming more lethal.

I am also indebted to INSEAD, and particularly Professors S. David Young and Deigan Morris, who invited me to visit, study, and teach. They then renewed the invitation, allowing me to return to Fontainebleau to complete the research and much of the writing and to collaborate with David Young on the contents. This collaboration resulted in a work that I believe is more accessible, understandable, and comprehensive than other books on the same subject.

I thank Harris Collingwood and Julia Kirby for championing the original article for publication in the *Harvard Business Review* and for valuable insight about framing our ideas to make them as concise, convincing, and useful as possible.

Jim Boyd at Prentice Hall was the first publisher to suggest expanding the article into a more comprehensive book. From the outset, it was clear that he was a supporter, a friend, and an insightful adviser. Those virtues became even more apparent during the writing process. Equally important, he has been a continual pleasure to work with.

There are numerous friends, Harvard Business School classmates, accounting and legal professionals, chief financial officers, and other business associates who provided valuable insights, leads, perspectives, and anecdotes. Thank you for your encouragement and your ideas. We tried to reflect them fairly in this volume.

My daughters, Amanda and Caroline, were extremely patient and encouraging as I commuted to Paris to advance the book development—they were even willing to listen to me use the family grocery bill to explain derivatives. Above all, I enjoyed the support of my dear wife,

Linda, who willingly manages around my idiosyncratic schedule and whose keen insights into the business world were an invaluable help as I grappled with issues of balance and content.

Harris Collingwood would like to make the following acknowledgements:

Thanks are due Nicholas G. Carr, who, when he and I were editors at the *Harvard Business Review*, first encouraged me to write about the corporate earnings game. Barbara Kellerman of the Center for Public Leadership urged me to accept the invitation to collaborate on this book. As usual, her advice was spot-on. At several crises in the book's composition, Deborah Ancona, Carla Tishler, Michael Tushman, and Marjorie Williams provided much-needed encouragement and support. Thank you all. The staffs of three Harvard Square landmarks, Leo's Place, Peet's Coffee, and Darwin's, kept me fed, fueled, and reasonably cheerful. A writer could not ask for better friends and neighbors.

Special thanks are due H. David Sherman and S. David Young for inviting me to work with them to turn their *Harvard Business Review* article into a book. Finally, to Katherine Blanco, for her unfailing kindness, unstinting support, and impeccable judgment, my boundless gratitude is insufficient, though it will have to do.

1

PROFITS YOU CAN TRUST—AND THE PROFITS YOU CAN'T

It was as if the world had turned upside down. For a dizzying stretch in 2001 and 2002, nearly every day brought fresh, front-page news of multibillion-dollar financial deceptions, spectacular bankruptcies, and executives in handcuffs. Public disgust grew with every sordid revelation. Yet just a few months earlier, business people had been celebrities, objects of public fascination, adulation, and envy. The CEO of Amazon.com, Jeffrey Bezos, was *Time* magazine's 1999 man of the year. Bill Gates, Jack Welch, and Warren Buffett were leading celebrities—when they entered a room, necks craned and flashbulbs popped, as if the men were rock stars and not the chairmen, respectively, of Microsoft, General Electric, and Berkshire Hathaway. Men such as Enron's Jeffrey Skilling, WorldCom's Bernard Ebbers, and John Chambers of Cisco morphed from obscure corporate executives to celebrated pillars of something called "the New Economy," a technological revolution that was going to generate more wealth than the world had ever known—and transform society in the bargain.

These and other executives were the heroes of a bull market in stocks of unprecedented strength and duration. In March 2000, the Nasdaq stock market index closed at 5132, climaxing a 15-year run during which it gained 2000 percent. From January 1999 to March 2000, the combined market value of just two corporations, General Electric and Microsoft, climbed by more than $240 billion. A staggering $309 billion flowed into U.S. equity mutual funds in 2000, up sharply from 1999, when the new-money flow reached $188 billion, and an even sharper contrast with 1990, when U.S. equity funds booked only $13 billion in new money. The market's seemingly insatiable appetite for new shares encouraged a record 554 companies to launch initial public offerings in 1999, raising more than $550 billion, more than 19 times the IPO funds raised in 1998.

American and foreign investors alike demonstrated their faith in U.S. corporations and American-style capitalism in the sincerest fashion possible: with their dollars. Business-school professors and market pundits alike assured them their money was safe in the United States—no other markets were so transparent, no other financial reporting system more rigorous or sophisticated, no market watchdogs quicker to sniff out deception and hype. Investors could trust the reports of strong sales and profit growth emanating from seemingly every company in those exuberant days. If there had been a problem with the numbers, someone would have caught it already.

According to this triumphalist ideology, the stock market was a perfected democracy, a radically egalitarian realm where barriers of wealth, education, race, and gender were erased by information that was reliable and equally accessible to all. A group of elderly ladies from Beardstown, Missouri, enjoyed a brief spell of renown as purveyors of down-home investment wisdom, while television advertisements for one online brokerage firm featured "Stuart," a multiply pierced, tattooed, pink-haired young man whose preferred form of self-expression wasn't rock music or performance art but stock trading. As much as their styles diverged, Stuart and the Beardstown ladies both embodied the late-1990s populist faith that amateur investors, armed with nothing more than common sense and a personal computer, could hold their own against highly paid professional stock pickers. In this best of all possible markets, everyone stood an equal chance to prosper.

That faith was shattered by a stock-market collapse that began in March 2000. There are many ways to measure the damage, starting with the estimated $16 trillion in market value vaporized in the slide. But how should we measure the loss of belief, the obliteration of confidence in the market's basic fairness? If the corporate scandals have taught us anything, it is that the U.S. stock market of the late 1990s was anything but a level playing field. The leaders of Computer Associates used dubious accounting to pump up the price of their company's stock long enough to earn themselves a $1 billion bonus; then they changed their accounting method and forecast a sharp drop in sales. Top executives at Enron frantically dumped their shares even as they urged the public and their own employees to buy the company's stock. Securities analysts at Merrill Lynch, probably America's most respected investment firm, routinely derided in private the stocks that they tirelessly hyped to the public. Accounting firms signed off on financial statements they knew to be riddled with errors and unrealistic assumptions, and law firms devised and abetted transactions that existed for no other reason than to lend a false glow of profitability to sickly enterprises. Investment bankers offered hard-to-get shares in lucrative initial public offerings (IPOs) to the senior executives of companies whose business they were soliciting. The New Economy's promise of small-investor paradise turned out to be as phony as the financial results posted by some of its leading companies.

The revelations of corporate dishonesty and executive excess have prompted an angry public backlash against business. Approval ratings of corporate executives briefly fell to levels normally visited only by journalists, members of Congress, and child molesters. Even Jack Welch, the former General Electric chairman who long enjoyed almost universal acclaim for his business prowess, came under fire for the lavish retirement package he extracted from GE and then renounced when the benefits were revealed in a court filing in his divorce case. Antibusiness sentiment reached such a pitch during the summer of 2002 that President George W. Bush, a Harvard MBA whose administration prides itself on its quasi-corporate operating style, found it politic to rail against corporate crooks. But as they searched for someone to blame, more than a few investors found themselves looking in the mirror and asking some hard questions. Could they have seen the train wreck coming? Were there red flags hidden in the corporate accounts, warning signs lurking among the figures and footnotes?

There were, in most cases. Not every piece of shady accounting was detectable to outsiders: WorldCom's shift of operating expenses into capital accounts was all but invisible to anyone who wasn't a party to the fraud. But various financial filings by Enron revealed—in opaque, convoluted prose—the existence of the "off-balance-sheet" partnerships that were to prove its undoing. The company's earnings report (known as the 10-Q, after the Securities and Exchange Commission form it's filed on) for the summer quarter of 1999 noted that Enron was doing business with a private partnership led by "a senior officer of Enron." A later filing identified that senior executive as chief financial officer Andrew S. Fastow, now under indictment for fraud. When a sharp-eyed reporter for the *Wall Street Journal* started making inquiries about the partnership, the company's financial fictions began to unravel, and its collapse followed with shocking speed.

Warning signs could also be found in the books of Kendall Square Research (KSR), a high-end computer maker whose deceptive accounting, revealed in 1993, presaged the chicanery employed by technology companies later in the decade. (In the chapter on revenue recognition we'll take a closer look at Kendall Square, its accounting, and the damage it did.) In its 1992 financial filing, Kendall Square reported annual sales of $21 million. At the same time it disclosed cash collected from customers of only $8.5 million. Ordinarily, sales and cash track closely together. When these two numbers diverge, it may be a sign that a company is booking sales too aggressively—that is, reporting sales that will ultimately realize less cash than initially claimed as revenue. Such was the case with KSR, which was reporting far more in sales than it could ever hope to recover from its customers. In June 1993, following an investigation prompted by a reporter's inquiries, KSR issued a revised report of its sales and earnings. The correction—known in accounting parlance as a restatement—showed sales of only $10.1 million and a loss that had expanded to $21.6 million from the $12.7 million originally reported for 1992. Following the restatement, KSR stock nose-dived, losing almost two-thirds of its value in a single day of trading. The company never recovered from the blow.

The warning signs were there. Investors missed them because of their avid and uncritical focus on corporate revenue and earnings as the sole determinants of market value. Knowing how lavishly investors rewarded companies that delivered steady revenue and earnings growth (and knowing how lavishly those companies rewarded their senior executives), corporate managers became adept at exploiting the vulnerabilities, ambiguities, and gray areas of the accounting system to produce earnings on demand. Priceline, an online shopping service that enjoyed a brief vogue during the Internet boom, promised consumers that they could "name their own price." Far more common in the 1990s were companies that named their own profits. Many continue to do so, even in today's more cautious and skeptical environment.

We hasten to note here that none of the accounting games we discuss in this book are confined to the United States. Just ask the French: The collapse of Credit Lyonnais laid bare a financial fraud that dwarfed even Enron, with staggering costs ultimately borne by French taxpayers. Accounting systems come in many different flavors, and they all offer wide scope for mischief. From Australia to Asia, from Moscow to Brussels, companies have collapsed and fortunes have been lost because of shoddy governance, executive greed, slipshod auditing, and overly aggressive accounting. Many of these collapses, and the frauds that preceded them, make the Enron and WorldCom debacles look like Sunday picnics. Because accounting trickery knows no borders, and because business is increasingly global, this book will include a generous helping of examples of deceptive or fraudulent reporting from both the United States and the rest of the world.

We note as well that most instances of inappropriate, overaggressive, or otherwise misleading financial reporting fall somewhere short of outright fraud. In fact, most financial frauds lie outside the scope of this book, which is concerned with accounting games that can be spotted with a trained eye. Fraud is by definition designed to escape detection, as the phony journal entries at WorldCom misled corporate insiders as well as outside investors, analysts, and regulators. This book can help you spot aggressive, self-serving, or misleading accounting judgments; outright fiction is far more difficult to detect.

This book is primarily concerned with the abuse of the discretion that managers are afforded under most national and international accounting systems. What makes Enron a mega-scandal is not that the company's managers, trained at places such as the Harvard Business School and McKinsey and Co., used their skills to distort the company's financial condition beyond all recognition. Company managements do that all the time. What makes Enron so sobering is that the company's funhouse-mirror accounting had the blessing of a prestigious accounting firm and a sophisticated audit committee. The financial scandals that emerged from the bursting of the New Economy bubble served to remind the public that the so-called fiduciaries who were supposed to protect their interests—corporate directors, legal and accounting

professionals, securities analysts and investment bankers—were instead
management's enablers, accomplices, and collaborators. The real lesson
of the scandals is that investors are on their own. If they're going to risk
their funds in the stock market, they're going to need to defend themselves. This book is intended as a general guide through the accounting
minefield for corporate executives, securities analysts, auditors, journalists, investors, and anyone else with an interest in corporate financial reporting. But for investors, especially, this book may have some
additional value as a self-defense manual.

Blast Radius: The Damage Accounting Landmines Do

The strategies and maneuvers that Enron, KSR, and others used
to name their own profits are examples of what we call *accounting landmines*—destructive devices buried in the books of corporations large
and small, well known and obscure. Like actual landmines, they may
never detonate—auditors, investors, and regulators may never discover
the deception, and catastrophe may be averted, or at least postponed. But
when an accounting landmine does blow up—when the markets learn an
auditor has uncovered a phony entry, or when a company can no longer
hide ballooning debt or "borrow" sales from future quarters—the explosion can blight businesses, portfolios, and human lives.

There might be little to lament if the wreckage included only
false-front enterprises like Enron. The fewer such outfits contaminating
the business environment, the better. But accounting landmines have
also taken down businesses such as Kendall Square Research, whose
computers were genuinely innovative and valuable. KSR could have
been a contender in the technology sector if its management had kept
honest books. Instead, KSR management played fast and loose with the
definition of sales, a strategy that was expedient in the short term but ultimately lethal to the company.

Like most of the other companies whose deceptive financial reporting we will examine in this book, Kendall Square took advantage of
the flexibility that is both the genius of U.S.-style accounting and its
greatest vulnerability. Accounting as practiced in the United States and
most of the developed world not only allows, it *requires* management to
make judgments about the future—about the likelihood that a customer
will be able to pay its bills, about the return a pension fund will earn in

the coming year, about the revenue a fiber-optic network will generate in twenty years' time. It is no exaggeration to say that there is room for mischief in accounting because *we cannot wait to see what the future will reveal*. Accounting allows us to make an educated guess—a prudent, conservative, honest guess—about the future. But it also allows us to make self-serving, unfounded, dishonest guesses, as Enron and KSR did. Books like this one may be useful, even necessary, in the battle for honest accounting, but they can never be sufficient. Ultimately, honest accounting requires corporate managers committed to giving investors an accurate portrayal of the health of their enterprise.

Honest financial reporting also requires vigilant corporate directors, lawyers, investors, analysts, and, yes, auditors, who are willing to look closely and skeptically into corporate financial reporting. Unfortunately, under the present system all those parties have powerful incentives to ignore or even abet deceptive financial reporting. Managers and employees want to retain their jobs and enhance the value of the options or share grants. Outside lawyers, accountants, and consultants want to preserve and enhance lucrative relationships with a fast-growing enterprise. Money managers and securities analysts want to see a share-price increase to keep their jobs and confirm the wisdom of their investment decisions. Venture capitalists want to make a killing, and lenders want to keep their creditor in business, if only because it's easier to be repaid by a going concern than by a bankrupt enterprise.

The bulk of this book will be devoted to the many ways the accounting system can be gamed to fabricate an inaccurate, misleading, or even fraudulent depiction of a corporation's financial and operational well-being. Accounting can be deployed as a kind of funhouse mirror, exaggerating some features of the business—its sales or earnings, for example—and obscuring others, such as costs, perhaps, or the extent of its indebtedness. There are many reasons why corporate managers would permit or encourage such distortions. Certainly job security plays a part: Managers who fail to "make their number"—that is, meet their sales and earnings targets—often find themselves out of work, or at least out of favor with their bosses, investors, and the business press. On the other hand, they stand to collect sizable rewards if they do make their number. But the motivation to cheat is not always selfish—or at least, not always personal. Managers distort their numbers to maintain their company's access to the capital markets, to meet lending requirements, and to gain an edge in recruiting.

But whatever the motivation, the end result is to send inaccurate, misleading signals to investors and the public at large. The distorted numbers produce distortions in the allocation of capital, steering money away from productive enterprises toward operations that go begging, once their true condition is known. Accounting games do further harm to the process of capital formation by driving investors, especially individuals, away from the stock market. Disgusted by the corporate community's failure to tell an honest story in exchange for investors' dollars, many individuals have abandoned the stock market altogether in favor of bonds, real estate, commodities, and other competing investments. Investor cynicism drives up the cost of capital for all businesses and shuts some of them out of the market entirely. What's more, the revelations of widespread corporate game playing make it difficult for companies to recruit the talented and trustworthy people that business needs to right itself. Investors and business people love to rail against interfering legislators and bureaucrats, but dishonest financial reporting may have done more to impede innovation and wealth creation than any law or regulation.

The Oldest Tricks in the Book

Sometimes it seems that accounting games came into existence around the same time as the Internet. Many of the most spectacular corporate flameouts of recent years were so-called New Economy companies: Enron, the "asset-lite" energy company that said it was creating a market for bandwidth; WorldCom, the acquisitive giant that would satisfy the supposedly endless demand for telecommunications services; Lernout & Hauspie, the Belgian developer of voice-recognition software that was to all appearances growing at breathtaking speed. At the same time that all three companies were reporting their most impressive financial results, they were collapsing from within, their management scrambling to sustain the illusion of a healthy business for another quarter. An emblematic instance of this scramble occurred in 2000, when the chief financial officer of Lernout & Hauspie traveled to the offices of the company's South Korean affiliate. His mission: to collect $100 million, which the Korean subsidiary reported as cash on hand. The parent company was facing a liquidity crunch, and the money, had it been real, would have eased the crisis. But as Lernout & Hauspie's

CFO learned, the $100 million was nothing but an illusion created by a massive accounting fraud. At that moment, Lernout & Hauspie's demise was inevitable.

The Belgian software maker fell victim to the same kind of deceptive accounting that had, over the decades, destroyed hundreds of companies. New variations on the old games sprang up in the 1990s—indeed, innovations in financial trickery sometimes seem to be the most lasting legacy of the New Economy. But even new-style accounting dodges such as EBITDA and pro forma earnings aren't really all that new. EBITDA purports to separate a company's cash earnings from its paper profits, but there is little evidence that it does and much evidence that it is highly susceptible to manipulation. So-called pro forma earnings amount to little more than an attempt to avoid the profit-reducing impact of expenses. (When he was chief accountant of the Securities and Exchange Commission in the late 1990s, Lynn Turner mocked pro forma profits as "earnings with all the bad stuff taken out.") As we shall see in a later chapter, both EBITDA and pro forma earnings had honorable origins as attempts to render a truer picture of corporate financial performance than could be obtained using conventional accounting. But in the 1990s, those alternative performance measures came to serve virtually no purpose but to whip up illusory profits.

Most of the other loopholes and ambiguities that the New Economy companies exploited were the same ones that rogue companies had exploited for decades. In the 1980s, Cascade International and ZZZZ Best defrauded investors of millions of dollars on the strength of wildly overstated revenue. Derivatives were the villains in several financial scandals in the 1990s, including the near-collapse of Metallgesellschaft AG, the venerable German metals firm. The value of assets such as inventory, plant and equipment, and receivables has always been subject to judgment. In the 1980s, the managers of savings and loans routinely overvalued their assets in order to stay in business and continue gambling with taxpayer money long after they were, in actuality, insolvent. The same sort of accounting kept many Japanese banks open in the 1990s, even though their assets were for all intents and purposes worthless. In short, as long as there have been accounting systems, there have been accounting games. What was different about the Internet bubble was the size of the incentives to play, which considerably broadened the set of companies in the game.

Although the New Economy companies didn't invent accounting trickery, they had many of the characteristics of companies that are more likely than others to succumb to the temptation to manipulate. Among those especially prone to push the accounting envelope are:

- **High-growth firms whose growth is slowing.** Rapid growth can be a company's worst enemy. Investors who pile into the company's stock when sales and profits are expanding every quarter are usually also the first to bail out as soon as results start to flag. Fearing a stock collapse, corporate managers may resort to deceptive accounting to mask a decline in their business.

- **High-profile glamor companies with extensive coverage in the business and popular press.** At bellwether companies like General Electric and Cisco Systems, even small problems attract widespread press coverage. Facing intense pressure not to deliver disappointing results, managers may view earnings manipulation as the lesser of two evils.

- **New businesses that engage in unorthodox transactions.** Businesses in emerging industries sometimes have unconventional ways of doing business, such as the advertising barter arrangements common between Internet companies. Traditional accounting standards, geared to more conventional exchanges of goods and services, may offer little guidance as to how to treat those transactions. Corporate insiders and outsiders alike must scrutinize the accounting issues raised by new businesses and new transactions. For example, should a computer-equipment supplier whose customers are mostly startups expect and prepare for more bad debts than a supplier that sells mostly to established businesses?

This problem will only increase as the Internet further blurs the line between manufacturers and middlemen. How, for example, should Dell Computer account for the sale of a computer monitor purchased via the Dell Web site but manufactured at and shipped from the plant of one of Dell's suppliers? Should Dell report as revenue the customer's full purchase price, or just its cut? Which party is responsible in case of a warranty claim? Does Dell need a new accounting treatment for this sort of deal? If it has adopted a new accounting treatment, is it suitable to the transaction in question?

■ *Companies in weak legal and regulatory environments.* In emerging markets and industries, where the central government and legal institutions are weak and corrupt, managers can often skirt rules and regulations with little fear of punishment. But the high-level looting at Tyco, Enron, and other companies shows that U.S. managers can be just as contemptuous of the law as the most cynical Third-World oligarch. Indeed, weak control systems may be harder to detect at U.S. companies, where efficiency and honesty at lower levels may obscure high-level corruption and greed. The core problem at Tyco, for example, wasn't with the financial controls employed by the conglomerate's many individual businesses. The control environment broke down in the senior executive ranks and at the board level, where managers and directors abandoned the disciplines practiced on the operating level.

■ *Companies that are followed by a small number of analysts.* Out of sight, out of mind: If a company's performance and financial statements receive little scrutiny from reporters, analysts, and sophisticated investors, managers may decide there is little risk to cheating.

■ *Companies with complex ownership and financial structures* that make key transactions less transparent and give rise to related-party transactions and conflicts of interest. Complexity is a dishonest manager's best friend. Enron didn't completely hide the existence of the partnerships that triggered its collapse. Instead, it obscured them in a barrage of information.

■ *Companies whose survival requires them to attract the next round of financing*. If a company needs to meet certain revenue or earnings targets in order to avoid technical default on its debt, the temptation to cheat "just this once" may be irresistible.

■ *Companies that strongly link executive compensation to short-term business goals.* Short-term goals such as sales, net income, or stock price generate intense pressure to make one or more key measures appear to be stellar, even when they may in truth be anything but.

The presence of these characteristics does not necessarily mean that a given company engages in questionable accounting practices. But the burden is on the management, directors, and outside auditors of these companies to subject their financial reporting practices to extra scrutiny.

Such scrutiny may not be forthcoming, however. Investors can no longer take for granted the honesty of those responsible for the quality and accuracy of a company's financial reports, not when some of the business world's most respected names—Merrill Lynch, Merck, Xerox—have been caught being less than completely forthcoming with the public. Reputation is no guarantee of integrity, as investors have learned to their cost. Enron's most dubious feats of bookkeeping legerdemain bore the seal of approval of Arthur Andersen, the accounting firm that was once the industry's gold standard for ethical dealing. No CEO, no board, no auditor is above suspicion, and no company's books can be considered off-limits to skeptical, aggressive inquiry.

Who Needs This Guide?

This book cannot produce the honest managers who will restore the public's confidence in corporate financial reporting. But it offers a defense against the less-than-honest ones. It is written for almost anyone involved in business—anyone who manages a company, serves on its board, audits it, analyzes it, reports on it, invests in it, or works for it. All have a stake in the integrity of the financial record keeping of the firm they're associated with. When two of us, H. David Sherman and S. David Young, broached the subject of accounting minefields in an article proposal to the *Harvard Business Review* in late 2000, we addressed ourselves strictly to corporate directors. The major stock exchanges had recently instituted a requirement that a minimum number of directors be "financially literate," able to understand a balance sheet, a statement of cash flows, and an income statement. (Regulators have never offered a satisfactory definition of financial literacy, which is one reason why U.S. accountants and regulators are now engaged in creating a different definition for board use: that of "financial expert.") The exchanges further decreed that those directors must be able to judge whether a proposed accounting treatment is appropriate for the transaction in question. Our idea was to develop a guide to the accounting landmines a financially literate board member ought to be able to recognize.

We broadened our ambitions after discussing our proposal with Harris Collingwood, then a senior editor at *HBR*. We agreed that we should not limit our audience to corporate directors. The finished article (H. David Sherman and S. David Young, "Tread Lightly Through These Accounting Minefields," *Harvard Business Review*, July–August 2001) was addressed to a much wider readership. Of course, we hoped the article would be read by corporate insiders—the "iron triangle" of managers, directors, and auditors responsible for preparing, reviewing, and disclosing a corporation's financial data. Without the ability to detect accounting landmines, insiders lack the skills required to fulfill their fiduciary duty to shareholders, creditors, pensioners, and employees.

But we also wanted our message to reach beyond the corporate inner circle. Collingwood had written a pair of articles ("The Earnings Game," *Harvard Business Review*, June 2001; and "The Earnings Cult," *The New York Times Magazine*, June 8, 2002) making it painfully clear that those on the outside depend even more than insiders on a guide through the accounting minefield. Lacking access to the data, debates, and deliberations that go into corporate financial reports, outsiders such as securities analysts, shareholders, journalists, and lower-level employees might be unable to uncover incontrovertible evidence of deceptive accounting. But they can learn to recognize where deception is most likely to occur and the forms it is likely to take. They can learn the areas of the balance sheet or income statement most subject to managerial discretion—and thus most vulnerable to managerial manipulation. They can learn to question the assumptions that go into certain numbers, and they can respond appropriately if those assumptions seem unfounded, self-serving, or otherwise at odds with reality.

The nature of that response depends on the position the outsider occupies. The securities analyst, suspecting the existence of an accounting minefield, can challenge management and raise questions in research reports—and in the process restore to the profession some of the skepticism and independence missing during the see-no-evil 1990s. Financial journalists can call their readers' attention to questionable accounting and ask corporate managers to explain their choices. In the process they can redeem some of journalism's failures during the 1990s, when too many reporters preferred to cheer executives rather than aggressively question them or their numbers. Shareholders can demonstrate their confidence—or lack of confidence—in management's financial reporting by speaking up at annual meetings, contesting the election of board members who lack financial literacy or fail to exercise it on behalf of shareholders, and selling the stock of companies whose management cannot explain clearly how the company makes its money or what it does with the cash. In so doing, shareholders could go some way toward atoning for their part in inflating the 1990s stock-market bubble. Employees can emulate Enron whistleblower Sherron Watkins and call management's attention to deceptive financial reporting.

As indicated by the date of our original proposal to the *Harvard Business Review*, we were pursuing this subject well before Enron's collapse in the fall of 2001, which ushered in the present era of corporate scandal. The continuing exposure of the rot within the U.S. financial reporting system has convinced us of the value of addressing readers who don't ordinarily pick up the *Harvard Business Review* but want to know more about the accounting chicanery that has produced so many headlines recently. In the present book we explain how accounting trickery works, show how it can be detected or inferred, and suggest how the financial reporting system might be improved. We hasten to point out that this book is not a treatise on corporate governance, a system for picking stocks, or a collection of advice for managers. It is not an introduction to accounting, though it assumes no more than a rudimentary knowledge of the subject. It is, simply, a guide through the accounting minefield for anyone with a stake in corporate financial reporting—and in one way or another, that includes most people of working age.

Regular readers of the business press will probably recognize many of the examples and illustrations we use in this book. As educators, we recognize that examples drawn from everyday life are a powerful teaching tool. And there has been no shortage of pertinent examples of deceptive accounting in recent years. We draw freely from press accounts, regulatory filings, and court documents, as well as our own experience in education, consulting, and journalism. The facts are a matter of public record; the interpretations and analyses of the facts are, of course, our own.

But can a nonspecialist really expect to understand the arcane complexities of modern-day corporate accounting? After all, understanding the financial statement of a corporation requires a grasp of the accounting principles, rules, and guidelines. It also requires familiarity with complex topics such as derivatives, pensions, taxes, goodwill, merger valuations, stock options, foreign-currency translation, and comprehensive income. Then there's the need to be aware of industry-specific transactions and the conventions for recording them. And as business becomes increasingly global, financial literacy requires awareness of the differing accounting standards that prevail in other countries—and for that matter, in different offices of the same company.

We do not presume to minimize the complexities of accounting, nor do we claim that this book will create expert financial sleuths overnight. We agree that the vagaries of various international accounting regimes significantly complicate any analysis. But our collective experience in academia, journalism, and business has convinced us that, just as in literature there are only five basic plots, there is a basic and quite limited repertoire of accounting games. For all their variety, the games fall into seven broad categories, and they take forms that anyone of ordinary intelligence and common sense can learn to recognize—in their outlines if not in every detail. You don't need an accounting degree, for example, to know that when a company reports $21 million in sales but only $8.5 million in cash payments from customers, something is out of whack. The discrepancy is sufficient in itself to prompt demands for an explanation. In fact, we propose a general rule when examining financial reports: If you can't tell how a company makes its money or when it gets paid, or how and when it pays its bills, it's time to start asking questions.

In the chapters that follow we will examine seven financial landmines—seven areas in a financial report where accounting mischief is most likely to occur. In largely nontechnical language we will describe the rules and principles governing each of the seven categories, and how those rules can be evaded, misapplied, stretched, or, in some cases, simply ignored. In each case, we will show how real companies—including

Coca-Cola, Enron, Qwest, WorldCom, and Xerox in the United States, Lernout & Hauspie in Belgium, and Metallgesellschaft in Germany— bent or broke the rules, fudged their numbers, and did grave damage to their companies, shareholders, employees, and ultimately the global financial system itself.

We will do more than offer after-the-fact analysis and explanation. We will also point out how to recognize accounting landmines *before* they explode. Where we see opportunities to improve accounting practices, we will point them out. There is certainly room for improvement. In the United States, alone, from 1990 through 1997, an average of 49 public companies a year filed earnings restatements. In 1999, the number of restatements more than tripled, to 150, climbed to 156 in 2000, and then leaped to 270 in 2001. Preliminary figures for 2002 indicate a staggering 330 restatements. Interestingly, 185 of these occurred after the passage of the Sarbanes-Oxley Act, which substantially increases the criminal penalties for financial reporting fraud.

Much as we would like to believe that dishonest financial reporting is a marginal practice engaged in by only a handful of "bad apples," the volume of restatements suggests otherwise. On the evidence of the recent accounting scandals and the explosion in restatements, we are forced to conclude that accounting gamesmanship is widespread. The stories in this book will go some way toward explaining why we discount the notion that the scandals were caused by a few overzealous managers—and why there may be many more scandals and restatements to come.

New Rules, New Reforms—But Will Anything Change?

The corporate scandals of 2001 and 2002 spurred Congress, the Securities and Exchange Commission, and the leading stock exchanges to press for reforms in reporting and corporate governance. In particular, outrage over the revelations of widespread, blatant fraud at WorldCom generated the political momentum needed to pass the Sarbanes-Oxley Act of 2002. That law requires, among many other mandates, that the chief executive officer and chief financial officer of every corporation publicly traded in the United States certify the accuracy of their company's financial statements and the adequacy of its financial controls.

Passage of Sarbanes-Oxley has unleashed frantic activity at the top of nearly every public company in the United States and at the many European and Asian companies whose securities trade in U.S. markets. One corporate director reports that the time he spends in audit committee meetings has tripled since the law's passage. Compensation committees are busy reviewing and revising executive-pay formulas. Financial officers are facing increased pressure, increased workloads, and increased visibility. Boards of directors no longer grant sweetheart loans to executives and fellow board members. Instead, they're issuing new guidelines covering everything from conflicts of interest to protection of whistleblowers. Regulators are issuing new rules that require corporate managers to include a discussion of critical accounting decisions in their annual reports.

Other rules will mandate the treatment of stock options as an expense and already require companies to explain in detail where their nonstandard, "pro forma" profit calculations differ from numbers reached using standard acccounting methods. United States accounting regulators are busy trying to close the loopholes that allowed Enron to move debt and losses off its balance sheet and income statement and into "special-purpose vehicles." Auditing firms are now required to rotate the partners leading corporate audits in order to prevent them from getting too cozy with corporate management. And the Securities and Exchange Commission has established a new Public Company Accounting Oversight Board (PCAOB) to review and improve the independent auditor function.

The PCAOB got off to an inauspicious start when the first nominee to head it was himself accused of being a party to deceptive accounting. Then, when the board finally held their first meeting, their first act was to award themselves annual pay of $452,000, or $52,000 more than the salary of the President of the United States. But the PCAOB may yet transcend its unsightly origins to become a powerful force for improved governance and accountability. Much depends upon the energy and innovative spirit of the board and its staff, as well as their ability to withstand political pressure. In these respects, they have much in common with corporate boards themselves.

But all this activity and effort, however laudable, will not put an end to misleading financial reporting. Attention to accounting standards may fade as companies return to profitability and growth—even though vigilance should *increase* as profits grow. And a surge in stock prices will once again tempt companies to fudge their numbers in order to keep up with their high-flying peers. Nearly 100 years of accounting policy making have not eliminated shady accounting practices—and not for lack of trying. When one salad-oil maker was found to have faked the amount of its inventory on hand, accounting rules were revised to require auditors to physically inspect inventory. Companies simply found new ways to deliberately misstate their inventory. When businesses discovered they could understate their indebtedness by leasing equipment instead of borrowing to buy it, the accounting rules were changed to require companies to account for such leases as debt. But instead of preventing companies from hiding their debt, the new rules merely forced companies to find new hiding places. The fact is, it is human nature to create systems, and just as human to devise ways to beat those systems. And no amount of reform will change human nature.

Neither will this book. What it will do, however, is give investors, directors, auditors, analysts, journalists, and employees one more tool for detecting accounting landmines. We will offer instructions for defusing those landmines. Defusing, alas, is not always possible, but at least we can improve your odds of staying out of harm's way when the mines detonate.

2

LANDMINES:
WHERE TO LOOK

L et's now introduce the seven categories of financial reporting where accounting landmines are most likely to be hidden. They are:

1. Revenue recognition
2. Provisions for uncertain future costs
3. Asset values
4. EBITDA, pro forma earnings, and cash flows
5. Risk management
6. Related-party transactions
7. Performance comparisons and benchmarks

We will examine each category in detail in later chapters. For now, we take just a quick look at how one company—Enron—distorted or even fictionalized the information it reported in each category. Enron seems the most appropriate choice for this brief exercise. Its bankruptcy filing isn't the largest on record, nor is its earnings restatement. But no company played a wider range of numbers games than Enron. Indeed, numbers games became its real business—executives at the company even thought of starting a subsidiary that would sell its smoke-and-mirrors accounting techniques to other companies. So it seems fitting that we should look for accounting landmines in its books, beginning with:

Revenue Recognition

Enron had several ways of making a molehill of revenue look like a mountain. A favorite revenue-inflating technique was to report the entire amount of a trading transaction as revenue. Let's say Enron brokered a trade of $1 million of natural gas—matching up buyer and seller without risking any of its own money on the transaction—and was paid a $50,000 commission for its trouble. Enron's standard practice was to claim revenue of $1,050,000 on the trade. Other firms whose primary business was trading—Goldman Sachs or Merrill Lynch, for instance— would have booked revenue of only $50,000 for a similar transaction. Such aggressive accounting was just fine with investors in the 1990s. During one stretch in 2000, Enron stock was priced at 70 times the company's per-share earnings, while at the same time Goldman Sachs shares were fetching only 20 times earnings.

Another way Enron distended its revenue total was to swap unused telecommunications capacity with phone companies such as WorldCom and Qwest, which were also desperate to pump up revenue to give the false impression of rapid growth. The companies would swap so-called "dark fiber"—fiber-optic cable that was in the ground but not activated—often without any exchange of cash. The companies would then each claim hundreds of millions of dollars of revenue based upon arbitrary and highly optimistic predictions of what that dark fiber would earn in, say twenty years' time. Enron and its telecom trading partners would account for the uncertain prospects of those assets as if they were a sure thing, claiming in one year all the revenue the dark fiber was projected to earn in twenty.

Could an outsider have known, or even had reason to suspect, that Enron's revenue claim had such dubious backing? For that matter, could an Enron insider have known without being aware of specific transactions? There was ample reason for skepticism. Remember our rule for reading financial reports: If it's not clear how a company is making money and when it's getting paid, it's time to start asking questions.

An analyst, a reporter, and certainly a corporate director would have been entirely justified in asking when the dark fiber would start to generate revenue and whether its estimated future value was in line with economic reality. And if an analyst or director had piped up to ask whether Enron's treatment of trading revenue was consistent with revenue-recognition practices at other trading firms, the company's game playing might have been exposed earlier.

Provisions for Uncertain Future Costs

We said earlier that problems with accounting creep in because of our wish to know the future. Nowhere is that more true than where companies face the question of accounting for uncertain future costs. Managers face many situations in which they know they'll have to pay out, but they don't know when or how much. They don't know how many customers will fail to honor their debts, for instance, or how much a patent lawsuit will cost them, or how many customers will ask for a refund, or how much a restructuring will cost. So managers make estimates. Theoretically those estimates should be based on historical data and reasonable assessments of the future. But other considerations can influence the estimation process.

Consider, for example, the quarterly earnings report. Although it has not been accused of doing so, Enron appears to have deliberately underestimated how much bad debt it would have to write off in 1996, in order to improve its net income. (Bad-debt estimates, like other estimated expenses, are deducted from net earnings.) From 1995 to 1996, Enron's accounts receivable increased by 65 percent, to $1.8 billion, while its allowance for doubtful accounts fell 50 percent, to $6 million. Very few companies find their bad debts falling by half as their sales increase by more than half. But then, Enron always said it was different.

Asset Values

By now, most readers of the business press know that so-called special-purpose entities (SPEs) with colorful names like Raptor and Chewco played a large part in Enron's downfall. They were equally important in Enron's rise. There is nothing inherently dishonest about special-purpose entities, also known as off-balance-sheet partnerships.

Pharmaceutical companies frequently set them up, forming partnerships or joint ventures with other firms to perform research and development, which usually entails high expenses and (in the early years, at least) low returns. By setting up a separate, independently managed research enterprise and sharing its risks and rewards with one or more partners, the pharmaceutical company can legitimately isolate an SPE's finances from its own.

But Enron used its SPEs as yet another device for naming its own profits. It would transfer assets, such as a contract to supply energy to a customer, into an SPE at a value that would allow Enron to claim a profit on the transaction. It did so using an accounting procedure routinely used by firms that trade in stocks and bonds. At the end of each trading day, those firms value their inventory of securities by using so-called mark-to-market accounting. That is, they value them at the last price similar securities fetched on the open market. Mark-to-market is the most reasonable way to value assets—as long as there is an active market for the securities or other assets in question. But no such market exists for power-supply contracts, which are complex, one-of-a-kind deals whose value is determined by lengthy negotiation. Nonetheless, using the discretion permitted them by U.S. accounting rules, executives of Enron marked the supply contract to market, selling it to the SPE at a price the executives estimated it would fetch in an open-market transaction. Since there was no market for such contracts, the executives set the value arbitrarily, usually naming a wildly optimistic figure that allowed Enron to post an immediate profit on the transaction. Even that maneuver might have passed muster if the managers of the SPE had been truly independent of Enron. But the managing partner of the SPE was also an Enron executive, with a strong interest in paying the highest possible price for the asset. Enron finally had to acknowledge that its SPEs were not truly independent and had to include their financial results in its own financial reports. At that point Enron's true and perilous financial situation became clear—or at least *more* clear—and its death spiral began.

EBITDA, Pro Forma Earnings, and Cash Flow

Enron's cash-flow statement for 2000 says that the company generated $4.7 billion in cash from operations that year, compared to $1.2 billion in cash in 1999. What should have aroused suspicion is that

Enron reported this near-quadrupling in cash without ever saying precisely where the new cash was coming from. Enron was inflating its trading revenue at the same time, and indeed was entering into trades simply to puff up its revenue numbers, and it seems likely that its cash-flow statement was subject to similar puffery. But the real point is that Enron's very unwillingness to state just how it achieved such an impressive increase in cash flow should have tipped off investors that there was more (or less) to Enron than met the eye.

Risk Management

Risk is an inevitable part of business, and effective risk management is a sign of a well-run company. Poorly managed companies such as Enron only pretend to manage their risks. One way Enron did so was to shift into its SPEs risky assets such as contracts to supply power at a fixed price. In fact, the SPE never truly assumed the risk of the power contract. Enron retained the risk, guaranteeing the SPE that it would issue new Enron stock to compensate the partnership for any losses it might incur on the power contracts. In other words, instead of shifting its risk to the SPE, Enron used its own stock to insure the SPE against risk. The scam might have gone undiscovered had the unthinkable not happened: The value of the power contract and Enron stock both declined sharply. Enron could not issue enough stock to compensate the SPE without severely diluting its stock and sending its price down even further.

Enron paid a heavy price for disguising its risks. Stock and bond investors can't make an informed decision to buy or sell without knowing what risks a company faces and how it plans to deal with those risks. When investors realized Enron had misled them, they not only bailed out of the company's securities, they refused to extend the company any help in refinancing. Disguising risks may have extended Enron's existence for a while but ultimately assured its demise.

Related-Party Transactions

Accounting rules require companies to disclose so-called related-party transactions. Such transactions include things like a company's using a limousine service owned by the CEO's brother, or its purchase of cleaning services from a company owned by a board member. Such transactions are not necessarily nefarious, although analysts, investors, and board members should be extra vigilant in assuring that the transactions are fully and clearly disclosed and that the prices paid to related parties for products and services are no more than reasonable and customary. But true to form, Enron withheld or obscured important information about the related-party transactions it entered into. Yes, it disclosed that its chief financial officer and other important executives were involved with the SPEs. But it did not disclose how much these officers stood to gain from the partnerships, or that they often stood to reap the largest gains by working against the interests of Enron and its stockholders. The vague and confusing quality of Enron's discussion of its related-party transactions was itself a signal that the company had something to hide.

Performance Comparisons and Benchmarks

Of all the accounting sins Enron committed, its lapses with regard to benchmarking were hardly the worst. But the inconsistent and self-serving way it used comparisons to other firms was indicative of the organization's culture, which seemed to revel in violating the spirit of accounting rules while appearing to uphold their letter. Thus, Enron billed itself as a trading firm for the New Economy, an "asset-lite" juggernaut that used technology and information to make trading markets in everything from bandwidth to weather. But it didn't adhere to the accounting conventions followed by other trading firms. As noted above in our discussion of revenue recognition, Enron recognized as revenue the gross amount of trading transactions, rather than the much smaller amount it actually netted. In doing so, Enron pumped up its apparent size to rival that of giants like Morgan Stanley or Merrill Lynch. But how much larger would those firms have looked if they had emulated Enron's method of revenue recognition?

In fact, by any honest measure, Enron was an underperformer. Its return on invested capital (earnings as a percentage of shareholder equity plus debt) was a modest 7 percent. Its operating margin (operating income as a percentage of sales) declined from an already-low 5 percent in 2000 to 2 percent in 2001. Yet the price-to-earnings ratio of Enron stock at times was as high as 70, while the shares of well-established, well-managed financial intermediaries such as Goldman Sachs were trading at 20 times earnings. Those who bought Enron shares at 70 times earnings (overstated earnings, that is) could not have been basing their decisions on present performance but on the company's assurances (echoed by its supporters in the media and on Wall Street) of a future of virtually limitless growth. Indeed, Enron is perhaps the perfect embodiment of the hype culture of the late 1990s, when promotion came to count far more than performance.

Early in this chapter we asked if there were any warning signs of financial disaster ahead. In Enron's case, there certainly were. (Indeed, a handful of investors recognized the warning signs and sold short or excluded Enron from their portfolios. They also advised others to stay away, though few listened.) A close analysis of any of Enron's accounting decisions in seven crucial categories would have shown that, even if the company met U.S. accounting standards, its reports did not completely and accurately reflect the company's financial condition, and thus they should not have been issued. Some of the problems were identifiable through analysis of the footnotes. Other problems were hidden behind opaque or incomplete footnotes and comments in the Management's Discussion and Analysis section of the annual report.

But that just begs the question: Why would anyone invest in a company whose financials were so hard to decipher? Investors acted as if Enron's profits would vanish if anyone inquired into them too closely. Come to think of it, that's exactly what happened. Unexamined by the company's directors and auditors, as well as its investors and analysts, Enron's misdeeds continued to compound and its liabilities continued to mount. Its accounting landmines exploded, one after the other, and it was forced to restate earnings. Investors quickly realized that the Houston trading powerhouse that billed itself, with a sort of grandiose vagueness, as "the world's leading company," was a chimera created by accounting trickery. They dumped their shares, Enron's doom was assured, and the long season of corporate scandals had begun.

The Global View—Is It Any Better Over There?

In the wake of the Enron disaster, investors and commentators around the world enjoyed a rare opportunity to turn the tables on the United States. During the boom of the 1990s, American executives and government officials had not been shy in lecturing the rest of the world about the glories of the U.S. financial system and the shortcomings of the systems of other countries. In particular, Americans trumpeted the vigilance of U.S. regulators and the transparency of U.S. financial reporting. So when the Enron fiasco hit the front pages of the world press, some outside the U.S. rather gleefully suggested that the scandal would never have happened in *their* countries. That is a dubious assertion. The key question for both insiders and outsiders, wherever they may find themselves and whatever accounting regime is in force, is whether the information companies provide is fair, understandable, reliable, and relevant.

Certainly no country can claim to be untouched by financial scandal. Serious accounting issues have been identified in firms around the world, including, in recent years, Gazprom in Russia, Postovni bank in the Czech Republic, numerous banks in Japan, and Vivendi in France. The UK's Cable and Wireless was accused of overstating revenues through swaps. And the Dutch grocery company Ahold appears to have engaged in widespread accounting fraud, in particular overstating revenue by falsifying supplier rebates.

Audit irregularities are also an international phenomenon. An external audit of Xerox's Mexican subsidiary overlooked overstatement of revenues. KPMG, the auditor of Lernout & Hauspie, found overstated revenue on the books of the software company's South Korean affiliate and questioned the entry but ultimately allowed it to stand. Much to KPMG's embarrassment, L&H later had to restate that revenue. KPMG auditors were also prevented from contacting L&H's customers, but the firm did not inform investors of this extraordinary restriction, which is a violation of U.S. and most international accounting standards. Price-WaterhouseCoopers (PWC) was accused of lack of independence in its audit of Gazprom, a Russian natural gas business. PWC, investors allege, disclosed company contracts with relatives of Gazprom's management only after public outcry. And BDO Seidman certified the financial reports of a Cyprus automobile import-export operation without ever independently verifying the existence of any automobiles or customers to buy them.

Whatever the weaknesses of the U.S. model, it also has unique strengths. The United States, for example, requires management's discussion and analysis of results, in which management explains year-to-year changes in profitability and discusses solvency and cash-flow issues. Few companies traded outside the United States provide similar disclosures. Likewise, the United States, unlike many other countries, requires disclosure of management's compensation and the method by which it is determined. Moreover, U.S. stock exchanges are often a powerful force for high-quality financial reporting. United States exchanges, unlike those in Europe, require corporate boards to maintain audit committees comprised of independent, financially literate directors. We believe it is likely that as globalization forces a convergence of regulations and conventions, many features of the U.S. model will be widely imitated and adopted around the world.

But no matter what regulatory regime prevails, the responsibilities of directors, investors, analysts, auditors, and employees do not change. If they have evidence—or even merely suspicions—of dishonest financial reporting, then it is time for:

- Insiders to reconsider serving as board members, auditors, or legal counsel

- Investors to consider a different investment

- Securities analysts to issue no opinion if there is no basis for evaluating performance

- Bond raters to ensure that their ratings reflect uncertainty about the business's revenue and earnings

But what are the telltale signs of accounting deception? Many accounting maneuvers are surprisingly crude and obvious, so before scouring the books for sophisticated and complex disclosures, look for the tricks hidden in plain sight. Has management reduced discretionary research-and-development spending? Has it deferred maintenance or slashed its advertising budget—evidenced by a sharp drop in maintenance expenses or selling, general and administrative costs? That exercise of managerial discretion will boost earnings in the short term but likely prove costly in the long run, as maintenance becomes renovation and R&D becomes a desperate race to catch up with competitors that didn't starve their new-product pipelines.

Changes in key financial ratios often signal accounting games going on beneath the surface. Gross profit percentages (sales minus cost of goods sold) are a key indicator of the health of most manufacturing enterprises. Be sure to scrutinize even very modest increases in this percentage. Has the company improved pricing and production or cost-efficiencies, or are the improved margins the result of tricky inventory accounting? Service companies don't report gross profit percentages, but they often measure themselves by net income or operating income as a percentage of sales. Sharp, sudden increases in those ratios can be the result of improperly capitalized expenses or the manipulation of reserve accounts. Especially suspect are sharp sales or profit increases achieved despite adverse economic conditions.

Management has the discretion to make sales more attractive by discounting or providing other incentives. But when do such maneuvers constitute aggressive merchandising, and when do they amount to channel stuffing? Are the revenues of U.S. automakers real or prematurely recognized when they are generated by zero-percent financing? The credit markdowns may produce record sales during a weak economy, but those sales may be offset by a decline the following year. The point is, corporate financial reports have to be scrutinized within the larger economic context.

Sometimes management misleads simply by making up its own definitions of key terms. For example, there is no fixed definition of income, giving management ample room to include or exclude the proceeds of asset sales, interest income or expense, and income or expenses related to legal settlements. Thus it's also important to consider financial reports within the larger context of a company's industry and competitors. Does the management of one company define operating profits in the same way as its chief rival? If not, why not? Is it because the comparison looks better when apples are compared to oranges?

In the chapters to come, we will show you how to answer those questions for yourself—because you won't find profits you can trust until you find answers you can trust.

3

REVENUE RECOGNITION: WHAT IS A SALE, AND WHEN DO YOU BOOK IT?

It's worth repeating: Flexibility, the great virtue of most accounting systems as practiced in most of the developed world, is also those systems weak point. Thanks to their flexibility, most accounting systems can measure the financial impact of a wide variety of transactions, from the simplest retail exchange of cash for physical goods to complex trades of intangible assets whose value and useful life are uncertain. But where there is flexibility, there is also ambiguity, and where there is ambiguity, there is the opportunity for managers to abuse the accounting system.

In honest hands, most accounting systems are up to the job of providing a reasonably accurate rendering of a business's financial performance. Accuracy, however, is not always the aim of those who manage a corporation or stand to gain from cooperating with management, be they board members or outside accountants, analysts or investment bankers. All may have an interest in manipulating the accounting system to produce a misleading, distorted, or downright fictional portrayal of a business's health and prospects. And when the manipulation starts, it usually starts with the recognition of revenue (also called turnover or sales). Of the 720 restatements of earnings from 1997 to 2000 in the United States, 376—more than half—involved methods of revenue recognition. Restatements to correct improper revenue-recognition methods were reported by 183 non-computer-manufacturing companies, 116 software businesses, and 77 computer-manufacturing firms. As cheaters like to say, everybody does it.

The restatements were necessary because the original financial reports fell afoul of at least one of the two basic requirements of revenue recognition. First, the revenue must be "earned," which is generally understood to mean that the sales process is complete. In the case of goods, legal title has been, or is on the verge of being, transferred to a willing buyer. In the case of services, the service in question has been rendered. The second requirement is that the seller has to be reasonably certain of collecting the money publicly claimed (or, in accounting parlance, *recognized*) as revenue. The history of accounting chicanery is in large part a history of many attempts—some of them more ingenious than others—to evade those two requirements.

One of the simplest revenue recognition games is also one of the most common. Essentially, it's an attempt to dodge a rule known to every first-year accounting student: Goods shipped on consignment cannot be booked as revenue. Neither condition of revenue recognition has been fulfilled—ownership and its attendant risks have not been transferred, and since the goods might not even be sold, there can be no certainty of getting paid. But those strictures haven't stopped some managers from using consigned goods to fatten the top line—that is, the revenue line—of the corporate income statement.

Sunbeam, the appliance maker run into the ground by Albert "Chainsaw Al" Dunlap, shipped barbecue grills to retailers during the fall and winter of 1996–97, even though consumer demand for outdoor cooking equipment is a strictly warm-weather phenomenon. To induce retailers to go along with the scheme, Sunbeam allowed them to defer payment until they had sold the grills. They were also assured they could return any unsold goods. As a final fillip, Sunbeam picked up the tab for the warehouses where the grills were stored for the winter. In short, the grills were sold on consignment. Nonetheless, Sunbeam accounted for them as if they had been sold in the last quarter of 1997.

Sunbeam's exertions, known generically as "channel stuffing" (in this game, a company stuffs its distribution channels with merchandise, which it then claims to have sold) added $71 million to the company's 1997 profits. The company later had to restate those amounts after Dunlap resigned from Sunbeam under pressure from the board of directors. In September 2002, Dunlap agreed with the Securities and Exchange Commission that he would never again serve as officer or director of another public company and paid $500,000 to settle the government's civil case against him. He also paid $15 million to settle a shareholder class action. As is usual in such cases, Dunlap settled without admitting or denying guilt, but had the charges against Chainsaw Al gone to trial, he might have faced much stiffer penalties, given the current climate of revulsion from CEO excesses.

Financially ailing, suffering from years of mismanagement, Sunbeam fits the stereotype of the sort of company that would resort to a crude scheme like channel stuffing. But even apparently healthy, well-managed companies such as BristolMyers Squibb have been caught at the same game. In 2000 and 2001, the pharmaceuticals giant boosted sales by offering discounts to wholesalers to purchase more drugs than patients needed. In the first quarter of 2002, when those wholesalers stopped building up inventory, BristolMyers Squibb's sales plummeted. In October 2002, the company restated its 2000 and 2001 results, a move that affected more than $2 billion in revenue.

Other revenue-recognition games are far more sophisticated than those played by Sunbeam and BristolMyers Squibb. Some are downright elegant. But the difference between channel stuffing and fancier methods of prematurely recognizing revenue is one of degree, not of kind. At bottom, most revenue-recognition games are variations on a few simple themes.

Truth or Consequences: Why Companies Cheat

Companies often attempt to pass off revenue-recognition games as mere differences of opinion. Accounting, they say, is full of judgment calls, and management, far from trying to inflate revenue, is merely making a judgment about which reasonable people can disagree. It is true that, in some transactions, the moment when revenue has been earned cannot be fixed with precision. Because the consequences of management's decisions about revenue recognition can be so enormous, though, managerial protestations of pure intentions sound more than a little disingenuous. One set of managerial decisions can result in revenue reports that suggest high growth and strong customer demand—the sort of reports that encourage bankers to continue lending and investors to bid up the shares of the company doing the reporting. Another set of decisions yields a revenue figure that suggests slow growth, grudging customer acceptance, dubious future prospects. The latter set may send investors a more accurate signal about the future of the business, but how many managers are going to opt for accuracy over optimism, especially when their compensation consists mainly of stock and stock options, which grow more valuable as the stock price increases?

That's why it's so important to know a company's revenue-recognition policies. For example, how does a company recognize revenue when a customer takes delivery of a product but makes payments on it over several years? One approach is to consider all of the revenue as earned when the product is delivered. But a more prudent approach is to consider such things as the costs of servicing and supporting the product. Are they incurred all at once, or are they spread out over the life of the product, so that they should be matched against the stream of customer payments? And what of the customer's ability to meet its long-term commitments? How should a software company treat a ten-year agreement to provide e-business support to a client that is burning through millions of dollars a quarter and has no product on the market, much less revenue on its income statement? In the late 1990s, many suppliers treated such agreements as sure things and booked the revenue as if ten years' contract payments had already been collected. To a large extent, the collapse in stock prices after March 2000 represented the belated recognition by corporations and their shareholders that much of the revenue so confidently booked during the boom times would never materialize.

In addition to deciding *when* to recognize revenue, managers have discretion to define *what* to designate as revenue. Suppose an auction business sells an item for $100. Of that amount, $5 goes to the auctioneer as commission. On its financial statements, should the auctioneer include the total amount of the sale as revenue and call the $95 payment to the item's original owner an expense? Or should it count only the commission as revenue and show no expense? Most accountants would prefer to treat only the commission as revenue. The auctioneer is merely a conduit for the payment from buyer to seller; the money it passes to the seller doesn't come from its own pocket. All the same, some Internet companies, recognizing the importance investors place on sales growth, took advantage of ambiguities in U.S. accounting rules to treat the gross proceeds of auctions as revenue, a procedure known as *grossing up*.

Companies get away with grossing up because there are instances where claiming the gross proceeds of a sale as revenue is perfectly reasonable and justified. The existence of a legitimate precedent creates a penumbra of "reasonable doubt" around more aggressive accounting moves. Suppose Dell Corporation sells, as a component of one of its PCs, a computer monitor it purchased from an independent manufacturer. Does it recognize as revenue only its gross profit margin—the difference between what it pays for the monitor and what it charges its customer? Or does it recognize the price of the complete PC as revenue, treating the cost of the monitor as an expense, just as Ford recognizes the full price of a car as revenue and counts as expenses the costs of the parts it purchases from outside suppliers? In such a case, Dell recognizes the full price of the monitor, and rightly so. But what if Dell were to arrange—as it often does—for the monitor to be shipped directly from the manufacturer to the customer? Should Dell include the monitor's selling price in its revenue, or only Dell's cut? In other words, should Dell's sales figures suffer just because of an efficient logistics arrangement? Or should the decision hinge on a legal question, such as who would be responsible if the goods were damaged in shipping? Dell has resolved the ambiguity by recognizing the gross proceeds of the transaction as revenue, since its money and reputation are at risk if the product is damaged in shipping or fails to perform as advertised. That's a far cry from an auctioneer laying claim to money that it merely funnels, risk free, from one side of a transaction to another.

Grossing up was one of the dubious accounting practices that became almost routine during the Internet boom, and no company indulged in it more enthusiastically—or controversially—than Priceline.com, the company that invited customers to "name your own price" for airline tickets, hotel rooms, and rental cars. In a 2000 quarterly filing, the company reported revenue of $152 million. Priceline arrived at that figure by grossing up—summing the full amount customers paid for those tickets, rooms, and cars. Like any travel agency, though, the company kept only a small portion of gross bookings—the spread between the customers' accepted bids and the price it paid to travel and lodging providers. In Priceline's case, that spread was $18 million, meaning that it claimed $134 million in revenue that it actually passed on to various providers, booking the payments as expenses.

Priceline's accounting policy prompted skeptical questioning from the SEC and some stock analysts. Yet Priceline persisted. Why? Perhaps Priceline's senior managers actually believed their public pro-nouncements that as "merchant of record" the company assumed all the risks of ownership. But there is another possible explanation: the re-wards that were lavished on companies reporting rapid revenue growth during the Internet boom. Investors paid stratospheric prices for the shares of companies that had never recorded a profit and weren't likely to do so in the foreseeable future. To justify this evident folly, many in-vestors took to valuing Internet companies on the basis of their sales, theorizing that "critical mass"—a large customer base—was more im-portant than profit. Grossing up was a cheap and easy way of showing sales growth. The few skeptics who complained that Priceline's grossed-up revenue reports wildly overstated the company's perfor-mance were told they "didn't get" the New Economy.

Grossing up is not a practice exclusive to Web merchants. In 1999, Professional Detailing, a New Jersey–based firm that recruits and manages sales personnel for drug companies, started counting as reve-nue the reimbursements it received from clients for placing help-wanted ads. In serving as a conduit between its clients and the newspapers and other media where the ads were placed, Professional Detailing was no different from an advertising agency that uses client funds to buy televi-sion ad time. No advertising firm would count the client funds as reve-nue—the agency is only a way station for the money, not its destination. Similarly, Professional Detailing had no legitimate rationale for treating as revenue the want-ad reimbursements from its clients. Its auditors de-manded that the company restate its 1999 results and report 5 percent less revenue than originally claimed. In less than a month after the re-statement, Professional Detailing's share price fell 31 percent.

Edison Schools, the ostensibly for-profit education company that has never made a profit, played a similar game with a contract to run the Philadelphia public school system. Edison booked $30 million in revenue from that contract, even though the company paid $21.3 million of the total straight out to teachers and other school personnel. To poten-tial sources of finance to the money-losing company, revenue of $30 million gives a far more favorable impression of the company's health and prospects than the more reasonable and accurate revenue figure of $8.7 million ($30 million less $21.3 million).

Of course, no discussion of grossing up would be complete without mentioning Enron, which treated as revenue the entire amount of the energy contracts it traded. As a result, Enron slotted in as fifth largest U.S. corporation on the 2001 Fortune 500 (published in 2002), with $139 billion in revenue, even though it had recently filed for Chapter 11 bankruptcy protection. If Merrill Lynch, number 36 on the Fortune ranking, had grossed up all the securities transactions it handled for customers in 2001, it would have reported revenue in the *trillions* of dollars—enough, obviously, to move Merrill to the number one spot.

MicroTragedy and Other Revenue Wrecks

Grossing up is just one of the tricks in the revenue-recognition playbook. There are numerous other ways of making sales appear greater than they really are. An instructive scheme was employed by Micro-Strategy, a producer of data-mining software that parlayed its deception into a brief run as a Wall Street darling, before a restatement revealed one of the era's defining accounting charades—at least until Enron and WorldCom came along.

In March 2000, MicroStrategy announced that it was retroactively changing its revenue-recognition policies and restating its revenue and earnings for fiscal years 1998 and 1999. Revenue, originally reported as $205 million in 1999, was reduced to $151 million. Similarly, 1998's revenue, originally reported as $105 million, was restated downward to $94 million. The 1999 reported profit of $12.6 million was transformed into a loss of more than $33 million; 1998's profit of $6 million was converted to a loss of $2 million. The day MicroStrategy announced the restatement, its stock fell 62 percent, obliterating $12 billion of market value. It kept falling uninterrupted for almost two months, quickly earning the nickname "MicroTragedy" from rueful investors. All told, shares fell from $333 in March 2000 to less than $20 in May 2000, at which time MicroStrategy faced at least three class-action lawsuits by shareholders as well as investigations by the SEC.

The reaction of investors to the restatement vividly illustrates the market's penchant for reading sales and earnings reports, for good or ill, as a gauge of the future. The restatement required investors to revise their view of MicroStrategy's prospects and thus the value they assigned to MicroStrategy's stock. But how had MicroStrategy managed to paint such a misleading portrait of the state of its business in the first place? It took advantage of the latitude managers have in deciding when to recognize revenue.

MicroStrategy sold its software bundled with multiyear consulting engagements. Its product was not simply a set of coded instructions to a computer but also the company's expertise in customizing those instructions to a client's unique circumstances. Payment to MicroStrategy wasn't a one-time affair but a stream of fees that flowed in over the course of the consulting deal. Rather than spread the revenue from the software sale over the life of the contract, though, the company recorded it immediately.

The SEC had noticed that aggressive revenue recognition was becoming the norm among software companies, and the agency had complained to some of them. The policies not only overstated a company's growth rate, the agency pointed out, they also violated a fundamental accounting principle: Revenue should be matched against the costs associated with it. MicroStrategy, for instance, incurred costs—consultants' and software developers' salaries, mainly—in the course of fulfilling its consulting obligations to clients. Since MicroStrategy was receiving periodic payments from those clients, it would have been a simple matter to recognize those payments as they flowed in and match them against related costs incurred in the same period. Instead, MicroStrategy immediately booked all the revenue a software contract would generate over its lifetime. The move not only gave revenue a swift kick, it sent profits into overdrive, since the company continued to recognize costs as they were incurred, rather than all at once.

MicroStrategy's outside audit firm, PWC, offered an opinion that the company's revenue-recognition practices conformed to standard U.S. accounting guidelines. A few months later, when regulators compelled the company to restate its results, PWC opined that the new numbers also conformed to U.S. accounting guidelines. If both statements are technically correct, then such assurances actually assure very little. In legal terms, according to a law firm that investigated MicroStrategy, the company's only questionable acts were to backdate a few contracts. Right—and according to prosecutors in the 1930s, all Al Capone did wrong was to evade income taxes. PWC paid $51 million in 2001 to settle its part of the MicroStrategy class-action lawsuit.

For a brief period, MicroStrategy's revenue-recognition game won it an enthusiastic following among investors and the business media. Of course, the game also ensured that there would be no future revenue to match against future costs, but that was tomorrow's problem. In the meantime, MicroStrategy stock soared. It had a growing base of loyal customers, thanks in part to PWC Consulting, the consulting arm of MicroStrategy's audit firm, which recommended the software to its clients. Company CEO Michael Saylor was lauded as a brilliant visionary—an assessment in which he publicly and enthusiastically concurred. Suddenly wealthy, thanks to the rapid rise of MicroStrategy's share price, he pledged to endow an Internet university that he claimed would rival Harvard.

MicroStrategy's newly won prominence, however, made it an inviting target to the SEC. The company's apparent revenue and profit growth was sending investors a wildly misleading signal about its condition and prospects. Its SEC-mandated restatement sent investors a more accurate signal, and they responded by radically revaluing MicroStrategy's shares. With shareholder lawsuits looming over him and the company he started, Saylor shelved his plans for an online university.

Investors' embrace of MicroStrategy, their willingness to believe the astonishing sales growth claimed by the company, had a strong element of wishful thinking about it. Speculators in New Economy stocks wanted to believe that the Internet had unlimited potential, and MicroStrategy's apparent prosperity, purportedly generated by brisk sales of software that analyzed Internet transactions, seemed to confirm that belief.

How Present Value Can Make Future Trouble

This brings us to an uncomfortable truth about accounting deceptions: They require a receptive audience—lenders or equity investors or analysts or investors who, for their own reasons, want to believe misleading numbers. Many such audiences are won over by a feel-good story or an appeal to fashionable ideas. The rhetoric of globalization, for example, provided a handy hook for a scheme by executives of Xerox to inflate the revenue from office-equipment leases.

When Xerox leases business machines such as copiers and printers to customers for extended periods, it treats the lease as a sale. It

books the value of the lease all at once as revenue, even though payments on the machine may extend several years into the future. In effect,
the lease is treated as an outright sale financed by the seller, and the periodic lease payments are treated as installment payments on the purchase price.

Under certain conditions, U.S. accounting conventions permit
this accounting treatment. The revenue booked is equal to the present
value of future lease payments. Here's how present value works: Say
you want to make an investment that will grow to $25,000 in five years.
Assuming a constant interest rate of 8 percent, how much principal must
you begin with to reach $25,000 in five years? The answer: $17,000
(rounded). That's the present (or discounted) value of $25,000, assum-
ing it's invested at 8 percent (the so-called discount rate) for five years.
Change any of the terms in that equation, and the answer can change
dramatically. For example, assume a discount rate of 4 percent, and the
present value of $25,000 leaps to $20,500. A change in management's
estimated discount rate increases the reported revenue on the contract in
this example by $3,500, or 20 percent.

The expansive effect of low interest rates on present value did
not go unnoticed by Xerox's sales personnel, whose commissions are
calculated as a percentage of revenue, or by Xerox's managers, whose
compensation depended on hitting revenue and earnings targets. In
1996, the company used a discount rate of 20 percent when booking
equipment-leasing revenue generated by its Mexican subsidiary. That
rate was in keeping with the high interest rates prevailing in Mexico at
the time and accurately reflected Xerox's own borrowing costs. The following year, Xerox calculated lease revenue based on a discount rate of
18 percent, a move arguably justified by a downward trend in Mexican
interest rates. But in 1998, while Mexican rates ranged from 24 percent
to 30 percent, Xerox slashed its discount rate to 10 percent, and the year
after that to 6 percent, although rates in the real Mexican economy
stayed much higher. Xerox attributed the growing leasing revenue from
Mexico to the success of trade liberalization in the region, not to its favorable present-value calculations.

Why would Xerox use a discount rate so out of line with prevailing interest rates? Remember how low interest rates boost present value,
and remember that Xerox posted the present value of equipment leases
as revenue. The lower the rate, the higher the present value—and the
higher the revenue Xerox booked. Xerox's questionable accounting

practices were not revealed until 2001, when the *Wall Street Journal* published a series of articles by reporter James Bandler. Bandler depicted a managerial culture that demanded revenue growth at all costs, and he quoted an unnamed employee of Xerox's Brazil subsidiary, who claimed managers there were playing the same revenue-enhancing games—indeed, the employee claimed the subsidiary would not have reached its revenue targets without the games. The articles also portrayed Xerox's outside auditor, KPMG, as deeply implicated in the revenue-inflation scheme, with audit partners showing the company how to maximize the revenue it could report from each lease. In 2001, following a lengthy investigation by the Securities and Exchange Commission, Xerox agreed to restate its revenue and income for 1997 through 2000 and pay a $10 million fine. Restated revenue dropped by $6.1 billion, and reported profits, which included a combination of revenue recognition and other reserve adjustments, declined by $1.6 billion. Xerox fired its audit firm, KPMG, replacing it with PriceWaterhouseCoopers.

Wrong Number: Telecom Tricks

The telecommunications industry had its own bizarre take on revenue recognition during the boom. From 1997 to 2000, Global Crossing took on over $7 billion of debt to lay 1.7 million miles of fiber-optic cable to transport data via the Internet. When completed in summer 2001, the network spanned 27 countries and 200 major cities around the globe. The company's debt load didn't seem to faze investors—Global Crossing's market capitalization reached $40 billion in 1999. But then other carriers entered the market, worldwide economic growth began to slow, and Internet usage, while growing fast, was not taking off quite as fast as company management had expected.

As a result, demand for Global Crossing's fiber-optic capacity began to wane. Fearing that deteriorating financial performance would cause its share price to collapse and call into question the company's ability to service its debts, management began concocting revenue from capacity swaps with other carriers. In one such swap, executed in the first half of 2001, Global Crossing "sold" $100 million of capacity to Qwest Communications, which was also suffering a demand slowdown, while "buying" an equal amount of capacity from the same firm. The $100 million price tag was an essentially arbitrary value placed on the transaction by executives of both companies. The asset they were trading was unused fiber-optic capacity (known in the industry as "dark fiber"), for which there was no demand and for which there might be no demand for years to come. Nearly 20 percent of Global Crossing's $3.2 billion in revenue in the second quarter of 2001 came from capacity swaps. For the first nine months of 2001, such swaps accounted for $600 million of Qwest's $15 billion in revenue. While the amount of the swaps appears modest as a percent of total revenue, it accounted for most of the company's sales growth in that period.

When the accounting treatment was questioned, Global Crossing defended itself by asserting that each leg of the trade was priced and contracted independently. But any reasonable interpretation of the deal would conclude that no real sale or purchase had taken place. Compounding the deception, Global Crossing, Qwest, and other telecom companies would record the sale of capacity as revenue without recording the offsetting purchase of capacity as an expense. Instead, the purchase was capitalized. Rather than being posted on the income statement as an expense, deductible immediately from earnings, it was listed on the company's balance sheet as a capital investment, its value being gradually reduced, or amortized, over several years. The maneuver increased reported profits by completely mischaracterizing the transaction, treating the payment of cash for capacity as if it were an investment instead of an expense.

The telecoms can no longer disguise the fact that they already have more than enough fiber-optic capacity, and so do all their competitors. They can no longer pretend that swaps of this useless, unwanted commodity have any real value, any more than they can pretend that the fiber-optic capacity they own is still worth what they paid for it. They must acknowledge the reduced value—or impaired value, as accountants say—by reducing their earnings by an amount equal to the decline in value of their fiber-optic assets. And since the SEC ruled fiber-optic swaps invalid in 2002, the telecoms must also restate previous revenue and earnings reports pumped up by swap transactions. For example, Qwest was required to reverse $950 million of revenue from capacity swaps.

Another game the telecoms played was to generate revenue unrelated to the basic business and claim it as revenue generated in the ordinary course of business. For example, Qwest would purchase networking equipment from Cisco, which it would then resell, at a profit, to KMC, a company that built and maintained such networks. Then, over the course of several years, Qwest would return most of that money to KMC in the form of payments for servicing the network supported by the equipment. Such transactions, which the company justified as a means of speeding network development, contributed to Qwest's sales growth, but it was quite a stretch to record their proceeds as revenue from the company's core business of selling telecommunications capacity.

Qwest had still more revenue-recognition tricks up its corporate sleeve, such as adjusting the publication date of its Yellow Pages directories to shift revenue from one quarter to another. In fact, as a general rule, it's safe to say that companies rarely play just one accounting game. Games tend to come in clusters, so when you spot one, remember the cockroach theory: If you see one, you can be pretty sure there are many more hiding in the dark.

Once again, don't make the mistake of thinking that revenue games are a purely American invention. The accounting firm Ernst & Young analyzed 41 UK software firms and characterized the revenue-recognition practices of more than half of them as poor or very poor. And in 2002, the UK-based Vodafone, the world's largest mobile phone operator, admitted to playing games similar to those played by Edison Schools and Professional Detailing. It booked all the revenue generated by wireless Internet services, even when it redirected a sizable portion of that revenue to third parties that actually provided the Internet content. Vodaphone's practice stands in sharp contrast to that of rivals MMO2, the mobile business spun off by BT, and Orange, the mobile arm of France Telecom, both of which strip out of reported revenues any amount owed to third-party content providers. In its defense, Vodaphone says that the payments made to third parties are treated as cost of sales—that is, an expense—leaving gross profit and other profit measures unaffected by the practice. Besides, says the company, the amounts involved represent only a small percentage of overall group revenues. Then why bother with the practice at all? One answer suggests itself: By inflating revenue relative to major competitors, Vodaphone can report higher average revenue per user, a statistic (or *metric*, in business-speak) closely watched by telecom analysts.

In response to the sort of gaming described in this chapter, the U.S. Securities and Exchange Commission in 1999 issued Staff Accounting Bulletin 101. The agency issues such bulletins from time to time to address accounting questions thrown up by a new sort of transaction or a new sort of business—or, as in this case, to rein in marginal practices before they become mainstream. In this document, the SEC staff declared that revenue should not be recognized until it is "realized or realizable and earned." To achieve this standard, all of the following criteria must be met:

■ *Persuasive evidence of a sales arrangement exists.* If a particular company relies mainly on written sales contracts, such a contract must be in place and signed by the seller and the buyer before revenue can be recognized. Not only must customers signal intent to buy the product or service before revenue can be recognized, they must do so in a manner consistent with company or industry practice.

■ *Delivery has occurred or services have been rendered.* In the case of goods, the risk and rewards of product ownership have been transferred and the buyer no longer has any right of return. In the case of services, the service has already been performed. Contractual obligations on the part of a customer to pay for services rendered or goods delivered *in the future* do not qualify.

■ *The selling price is fixed or determinable.* Without such a price, there is no reasonable basis upon which to measure the amount of revenue to be recognized.

■ *Collection is reasonably assured.* It should go without saying, but selling to a customer who might not have the financial means to pay is not a proper sale.

The SEC's bulletin didn't just come out of the blue, of course. The agency's staff prepared it specifically in response to the gross abuses of revenue-recognition rules that proliferated during the Internet boom.

One of the most dangerous accounting games is played with a method known as "percentage of completion." Popular in the construction industry, though used elsewhere, too, it allows companies to recognize revenue gradually over the life of a long-term project, instead of waiting, sometimes for years, until the project is complete. For example, if the total revenue to be earned from the project is expected to be $20 million, and 30 percent of the work was done this year, $6 million of revenue would be recognized in this year's income statement. While this approach has important conceptual merits, it is widely subject to abuse.

Percentage-of-completion accounting found its way into U.S. news in 2002, when Halliburton was accused of abusing the rules during the period when the Vice President of the United States, Richard Cheney, was CEO of the oilfield services firm. Like other firms with large, multiyear contracts, Halliburton recognizes revenue and profit on a percentage-of-completion basis. Since projects that run for several years often encounter unexpected costs, most contracts have cost-over-run provisions, which allow firms like Halliburton to increase their fees, as long as they can document the increased costs and win client approval. Until Cheney's tenure as CEO, Halliburton accounted for possible overruns in the most cautious and conservative manner possible, recording the increased fees only when the customer had explicitly agreed to pay them. But under Cheney, Halliburton adopted a new policy, recognizing fee increases as long as customer consent was merely anticipated. Most customers eventually approved the increases, but Halliburton's haste to recognize revenue and profits in advance of customer approval raised questions that the company was using the accounting change to dress up its income statement. Its merger with Dresser Industries was pending, and improved financial results would help Halliburton extract the best possible terms for the deal.

Local Customs: Industry-Specific Revenue Games

Each industry has its own special ways of accelerating revenue recognition. In the software business, companies have been known to book revenue from upgrades that have not even been produced yet, much less provided to the customer. While one might concede that some judgment is required to establish revenue-recognition policies in such businesses, it should be clear to managers and auditors alike that revenue can never be recognized until it is earned. And how can revenue be earned when the product supposed to generate revenue does not even exist?

The soft-drink industry has a few games of its own. One of the authors heard about one from a former chief financial officer of a large Coca-Cola bottler in South America. Whenever Coca-Cola wanted to boost sales in the country, it would ship massive quantities of concentrate to the bottler. It even kept refrigerated trailers on the bottler's premises for just such an occasion. The bottler incurred no obligation to Coca-Cola until it was ready to use the concentrate. Thus, while the concentrate was physically transferred and invoiced to the bottler, none of the unordered quantities were included in its inventory, and it was not expected to pay any interest to Coca-Cola on the unpaid invoice. The sole purpose of the practice was to allow Coca-Cola to artificially boost revenue, practically at will.

Why haven't Coca-Cola's auditors pointed out this transparent charade and demanded that the company put a halt to it? The answer is unclear, but it may be worth pointing out that the same firm that audits Coca-Cola worldwide, Ernst & Young, also audits the South American bottler.

Another common ruse, found in many industries, is to misclassify the gains that arise from selling off valuable real estate and other corporate assets. Such one-time gains should clearly be segregated from regularly recurring revenue and, if large enough, reported as separate line items on the income statement. But some companies try to classify one-time gains as operating income. This maneuver is not reserved for marginal, fly-by-night operations. In 2002, IBM received embarrassing press for trying to pass off as operating income a $300 million gain from the sale of a business. To cynical minds, it appeared that IBM was trying to fool investors and bankers into believing that the company's underlying, day-to-day business operations were more profitable than they really were.

Back when the stock market was throwing money at anything Internet related, Web site operators played a game they called "concurrent transactions." For centuries, the word "barter" sufficed to express the same concept. In a concurrent transaction, two companies would trade banner spots on each other's Web site, recording the deal as both revenue and expense. The net effect on profit was zero, but at least the companies could report revenue to convince investors that there was some substance to their business. GAAP forbids this practice except under highly restrictive conditions, but many Internet businesses did it anyway, and few analysts, investors, or regulators called them on it. Nor has the practiced died out with the dot-coms. Siebel Systems took a big hit in its share price in 2002 when investors realized that nearly one-fifth of the software developer's second-quarter revenue came from concurrent transactions, a big number in itself and a sharp increase from the second quarter of 2001.

There are real costs associated with adopting revenue-recognition policies so aggressive they must eventually be reversed. In October

2000, the UK's Cedar Group, which was trying to bring a stock offering to market, received unfavorable media attention for its revenue-recognition policies. With investors uncertain about the company's true value, the company's shares lost a third of their value. The underwriters that were handling Cedar Group's stock offering found themselves holding shares for which they'd paid a 28 percent premium above market price. Cedar subsequently adopted revenue-recognition policies consistent with U.S. standards, transforming an 8.5-million-pound profit into a 24.4-million-pound loss.

A small amount of revenue manipulation can have a substantial impact. In 2000 and 2001 AOL recorded $190 million in revenue that was really nothing more than advertising fees paid by some of AOL's own divisions—garden-variety intercompany transfers of funds, which are, of course, not revenue. The revenue was minuscule relative to the company's overall revenue, but by recognizing it when it did, AOL was able to report that ad revenue was growing just as it was preparing to acquire Time Warner. By misrepresenting the state of its business, AOL was able to extract more favorable terms from Time Warner than it could have otherwise. Indeed, had Time Warner known the true state of AOL's business, the deal might not have gone through at all.

Nagging Questions: What to Ask the CFO

Clearly, the rules governing revenue recognition allow plenty of scope for all sorts of game playing—and whenever regulators or vigilant investors close off one loophole, another opens up. No corporate director, analyst, audit partner or investor can be sure of spotting every game. They can, however, ask questions and listen carefully to the answers for any hint of evasion, euphemism, or an attempt to change the subject. It's not necessary to know every detail of a game to know that games are being played and to react accordingly, either by selling shares or by contacting the chief financial officer or head of the audit committee and demanding an explanation. Don't trust your money or your reputation to a company that can't give a straight, comprehensible answer to one or more of these questions:

- How is revenue defined? And what event triggers its recognition?

- Does the company's revenue-recognition policy present a reasonable measure of the revenue earned by the business during the reporting period? Is it consistent with revenue measures used by domestic and global competitors? And is it clearly described in the financial statement footnotes?

- If revenue is measured in an unusual or new way, is that disclosed? Changes in methods of measuring revenues require careful scrutiny. Are new revenue streams measured in a manner that reflects the risk and nature of the sales? The footnote on lines of business and the geographic distribution of earnings, assets, and revenues always deserves careful scrutiny by investors.

- For a new industry or for a business beginning to sell to a different set of customers, a different region of the world, or different industries, what is the appropriate method of measuring revenue? Are the company's existing methods really sufficient and appropriate? Will the answer be the same if the new customers, regions, or industries become the predominant source of revenue? Would the company's revenue-recognition policies bear up under front-page scrutiny by the financial press?

- Where revenue substantially exceeds cash received, are there clear business reasons that explain the divergence? If receivables are growing rapidly, has the company made adequate allowances for nonpayment?

- Are the individuals who evaluate and report on corporate revenue policies knowledgeable and independent? Are the people responsible for audits of fast-growing divisions and subsidiaries applying the same audit standards required of head-office auditors? Are the qualifications of those auditors sufficient, or are additional procedures needed to ensure the reliability of the financial statements?

■ What would be the impact on net income if alternative revenue-recognition methods were applied? If the results would be substantially different, what are the implications for benchmarking, investor and bond-rating analyses, and executive compensation? Would the conclusions of this analysis suggest adoption of different recognition methods?

■ Are the changes in revenue from quarter to quarter and year to year consistent with management's expectations and the industry environment? Is revenue growing at a time when the industry is stagnating or even declining? If so, what enables the business to run counter to the industry norm?

That last question is crucial. Don't trust any corporation that says, in effect, "Trust me," when asked the source of outsized revenue or profits.

As we have emphasized, for every stream of revenue coming in, there should be a related stream of expenses flowing out. Given that many corporate managers commonly resort to games to pump up revenue or book it sooner, is it likely that they'd also play games to make expenses look smaller than they really are? What do you think? In the next chapter we'll look at the many creative ways in which dishonest companies may hide their costs.

4

PROVISIONS AND RESERVES: WHEN REVENUE GAMES AREN'T ENOUGH

It's worth repeating: There is room for mischief in accounting because *we can't wait to see how things turn out*. If a company were to shut down one of its factories today, the full cost of the shutdown would not be known for two years or more. But under U.S. and international accounting conventions, that company would nonetheless be required to estimate the final costs of closing—taking into account severance payments to employees, fees paid to dispose of plant and equipment, inventory write-offs, and many other expenses—and list them as a charge against earnings on its income statement. Those charges would also appear on the balance sheet in a liability account, usually under a heading such as "provisions" or "other liabilities." The numbers in those accounts are supposed to be a company's best guess of expected future obligations. Many times they are. But sometimes those numbers are a means of making earnings look larger than they really are. At other times, they represent a sort of rainy-day fund, to be drawn upon when profits dwindle.

Expenses, of course, are bound to arise in the regular course of business. But the precise amount and timing of some expenses can't be known in advance. Inventory becomes obsolete; some bills can't be collected; some customers return goods, others exercise warranties; environmental damage needs to be cleaned up; severance is paid; defective goods are recalled. Companies are required to estimate those future expenses, so that company managers and investors can form some idea of future claims on each company's cash. But rather than give their good-faith best estimates, some companies treat the expense categories of their financial reports primarily as an earnings-adjustment mechanism. And they do so with at least the tacit approval of directors, auditors, investors, and financial journalists. At such companies, provisions for uncertain future costs constitute an accounting minefield of potentially massive proportions.

In recent years, the poster child for misleading expense disclosure in the United States has unquestionably been Xerox. The copier company's financial reports in the mid-to-late 1990s bristled with expense figures that misrepresented Xerox's costs and deceptively portrayed the company's financial health and the success of its global growth strategy. Many of the most egregious instances of deceptive expense reporting occurred at Xerox Mexico. To meet aggressive sales targets set by the company's senior executives, lower-level managers of the subsidiary extended credit on generous terms to customers whose ability to repay was dubious at best. In the short term, Xerox's Mexican revenue showed impressive growth, but that growth came at a high price—some $127 million in bad debts. To avoid recognizing those bad debts, the managers of the Mexican subsidiary extended the due dates of the obligations, a maneuver akin to rouging the cheeks of a corpse.

By understating expenses and engaging in other accounting games (such as using leasing transactions to inflate revenue, as we saw in Chapter 2), Xerox was for a time able to report higher revenue and profits. The company in 1998 reported $585 million in profits from continuing operations. More than 20 percent of those profits were conjured by accounting trickery, rather than by actual commercial activity. But in 2001, a former assistant treasurer of Xerox blew the whistle, exposing the company's dubious accounting in the pages of the *Wall Street Journal*. The *Journal*'s coverage revealed that in addition to extending credit to uncreditworthy customers, managers of Xerox's Mexican subsidiary secretly rented warehouses to stash $27 million in returned merchandise—$27 million that should have been posted on the balance sheet as a liability and on the income statement as an expense. After initially pooh-poohing the newspaper's account, Xerox in effect admitted the charges were correct. It restated all its financial reports from 1997 through 2000, reducing revenue by $6 billion and earnings by $1.4 billion. The SEC censured the company and fined it $10 million. Wall Street imposed its own punishment: Xerox's market value declined from $46 billion in 1999 to $6.6 billion in January 2003.

While Xerox was churning out essentially fictional financial reports, its outside audit firm was KPMG. The accounting firm did resist some of Xerox's most outlandish accounting strategems, such as "Project Mozart," a bid to create a partnership where the company could dump some of its losses, but many investors and regulators hold KPMG at least partly responsible for Xerox's lax reporting standards. So does Xerox, for that matter. It has sued KPMG for failure to perform its fiduciary duty, adding to the legal woes of the venerable accounting firm, which was already facing a class-action suit filed by angry Xerox investors. And an investigation by the Securities and Exchange Commission is likely to result in sanctions, fines, and more damaging publicity for KPMG. Xerox illustrates perfectly what we mean when we say that accounting landmines have a wide blast radius.

Trips to the Cookie Jar:
Expenses Today, Earnings Tomorrow

Like many companies, Xerox *understated* its expenses to report higher short-term profits. But perhaps as frequently, companies will *overstate* expenses. Such overreporting often goes overlooked, because auditors and analysts are more vigilant about seeking out maneuvers that will inflate profits than about spotting attempts to reduce them. That's understandable: Injured investors are more apt to sue following reports of overstated earnings, claiming that the overstatement inflated stock prices to unsustainable levels.

Overprovisioning—and hence, underreporting—may be the quintessential accounting landmine, because, like real landmines, it is easily overlooked and has the potential to do great damage. Imagine an American widget company that has had a bad 2001; global widget demand has slipped and management will have to report a $5 million annual operating loss. Recognizing that the company has excess manufacturing capacity, management also decides to close its Canadian plant, a move that the company's top executives estimate will entail costs of about $20 million.

A gloomy picture, indeed. But management apparently decides that it's not gloomy enough. When the company announces its 2001 results, it reports a $5 million operating loss and also announces that it's taking a *$30* million charge to cover the expenses of closing the Canadian plant. (The language a company uses to describe the charge may vary somewhat: Rather than say it is taking a charge, the company might announce a $30 million provision, or create a $30 million reserve. But the differing words describe the same accounting maneuver.)

Why on earth would corporate managers exaggerate the costs they expected to incur by closing the Canadian plant? Their strategy is not as irrational as it may first appear. As we shall see, the inflated expense provision is a sort of investment—a $10 million investment in higher reported earnings, to be redeemed at management's discretion.

Here's how inflated expenses today translate to inflated profits tomorrow. Let's assume that a year after the closing of the Canadian plant, management's initial, lower estimates turn out to be substantially correct—the costs of closing the plant amounted to $20 million. By creating a $30 million provision for plant-closing expenses in 2001, the company in effect overcharged itself by $10 million. Accounting rules permit corporations to reverse those overcharges as they become apparent. The reversal shows up as a gain—a $10 million gain, in the case of our hypothetical widget maker—in net income. That extra income can make a good earnings report look great—especially when compared to the previous year's loss (a loss that was, of course, exaggerated in the first place by the excessive provision for future costs).

The widget maker's $10 million in excess expense provisions might have been an honest mistake. But it could also have been another example of management's cleverly using its discretion to present a misleading portrayal of its finances. In fact, this particular abuse of discretion has become so common among corporations that the charges have been given their own nickname: "cookie-jar" reserves (also known, especially in Europe, as "hidden" reserves). The idea is that the company overprovisions, putting cookies (i.e., future profits) in the cookie jar, and dips into the jar to boost profits in a later period. No cash is involved; expenses—and consequently profits—are ratcheted up and down merely by means of accounting entries reflecting management's estimates.

Why would the managers of our hypothetical widget maker willingly overstate expenses by $10 million, and thus worsen an already ugly loss? They're making a judgment about investor psychology. Investors tend to handle the shock of a large loss better if they think that the loss is largely attributable to one-time events—like a plant closing—rather than continuing operations. Thus the value of a big one-time provision has a multitude of uses: It can divert attention away from poor operating results. Such provisions can also give management an unearned reputation for candor—the company's leaders are supposedly making a clean breast of bad news, after all. And the provisions can serve as a sort of profits piggy bank, to be drawn on as needed.

Pharmacy chain Rite Aid was especially bold about creating cookie-jar reserves. In 1997, it earned a profit of $82.5 million from the sale of 189 stores to a unit of retailer J.C. Penney Co. But instead of following U.S. accounting rules and recording the profit as a one-time gain on its 1997 income statement, Rite Aid used the money to fund an internal reserve account that it used to absorb operating expenses and thus inflate operating income. That maneuver, as well as a whole host of other accounting dodges, came to light in 1999 after Rite Aid's share price collapsed. Early in 2000 Rite Aid announced downward revision of about $500 million of earnings for the three prior years, wiping out half its reported pretax earnings for that period. In the wake of several lawsuits, the company later reached a $200 million settlement with investors.

The Dirt on Big Baths

If cookie-jar reserves are such a widely known dodge, why do outside auditors and corporate audit committees allow corporate managers to create them? Part of the answer is that even the best-informed auditors and directors know less about the business than management, whose judgment is therefore accorded great weight. Directors and auditors may question management aggressively, but they are essentially in a reactive mode—they are probing for holes and weaknesses in a story that management has developed for its own purposes. Management can collect the evidence that will support its position and omit evidence that undermines it. Outside auditors and independent directors may be able, even obliged, to challenge management's case, but they may have difficulty obtaining contrary information or even knowing what to look for.

Mergers and acquisitions are another source of reserves that can be used to enhance profits in later years. When two companies combine, they create a reserve to cover expenses related to the process: severance and relocation payments; new stationery, business cards, and signs; information-systems integration; and a wide range of other items. Into this reserve, management often dumps every white elephant in the corporate cupboard, every failed scheme and wasted effort. Such "big baths" serve many purposes for a newly combined company. For one thing, the provisions make even weakly positive results in subsequent periods look good by comparison. And just as with the plant-closing reserve discussed earlier, overestimates of future expenses can be reversed to create profits when needed.

Big baths can also be used—or misused—to inflate operating profits and profit margins. An executive at one of the 1990s' most takeover-happy corporations charged $600,000 in travel costs to a merger reserve, even though the expenses were for ordinary business travel. By stuffing travel bills run up in the ordinary course of business into an account intended to hold one-time, merger-related costs, the executive was able to plump up his division's operating profits—that is, profits derived in the ordinary course of business. The more expenses can be shifted from ordinary operating accounts into one-time reserves, the higher operating profits and operating profits margins will be. This executive's compensation, it should be pointed out, depended on the attainment of certain profit targets.

Some big baths aren't big enough. Or so says the chief financial officer of a large U.S. bank, who oversaw one of the largest bank mergers of the 1990s. He confirms that bank executives, like other executives, engage in big-bath accounting after a merger, rooting out as many problems as possible and "fixing" them with reserves. But the reserves last only so long. For perhaps two or three years the reserves can absorb the costs of meshing the two operations, but eventually the well runs dry. The reserve is used up, and any further costs become operating expenses. Earnings decline—the opposite of what the merger was supposed to achieve. At this painful juncture, a short-term remedy presents itself to management: another merger. The merger reserve is replenished, and the cycle begins again. This CFO suggests that banks' acquisition strategies can be determined by the state of their reserve balances—as they decline, the chances of a new merger or acquisition increase.

As a general rule, companies are eager to highlight reserves when they're created, but far less eager to draw attention to the reversal of a reserve. Heinz, the food company, overestimated the costs of a 1997 restructuring by $25 million. When it subsequently reversed the overcharge, it did not disclose the fact on the face of its income statement, allowing the adjustment to enhance operating income. The SEC rapped Heinz's knuckles for the omission, requiring the company to make an embarrassingly belated disclosure of the reversal. In 1999, the agency took sterner action against W.R. Grace for a similar failure to note the reversal of a reserve, suing the company for fraud. W.R. Grace ultimately settled with the SEC in 1999, paying a $1 million fine and contributing $1 million to advance education about financial statements and accounting principles. But there is no telling how many such reversals the SEC failed to catch—the relatively harsh punishment meted out to Grace suggests the agency was trying to set an example to deter imitators.

Companies can also send misleading signals about the frequency of restructuring and plant-closing reserves and similar provisions. Such charges are segregated from recurring items on the income statement precisely because they are supposedly one-time expenses unrelated to ordinary, everyday costs of doing business. The idea is to isolate the impact of nonrecurring items on net income, thus delivering a better-focused picture of normal, recurring business activities. But what happens when restructuring charges themselves become a normal, recurring cost? In the early 1990s, before it was absorbed into Compaq, Digital Equipment reported restructuring expenses for three consecutive years. How can such regularly recurring costs be considered "extraordinary"? More recently, Motorola developed a well-deserved reputation for playing this game, reporting supposedly one-time losses for three consecutive years.

The Smoothing Game

The abuse of provisions for future costs is an international phenomenon. German companies are notorious for using provisions to smooth earnings, overprovisioning in good years to create the reserves that allow for higher profits in poor or mediocre years. The result is a stable earnings stream that's sharply at odds with the volatility of the underlying businesses.

Many German executives and some of their American counterparts would counter that such "income smoothing," as it's called, is not necessarily a bad thing. They contend that managers are better informed about their companies' prospects and long-term earnings trend than investors. Special events or temporary conditions can cause near-term results to deviate significantly from this long-term trend. By using provisions to smooth out the "noise" from these special events, corporate managers argue that they are, in fact, giving investors a clearer view of the company's future earnings potential and a better basis for the pricing its shares. Such earnings management, executives say, is really for the benefit of shareholders.

Even General Electric, arguably the world's most admired company, is known to play the income-smoothing game. GE is, famously, a highly diversified company, doing business in lighting, appliances, power generation, medical systems, engines, and financial services. This naturally gives it a more stable earnings stream than more tightly focused companies, especially those in cyclical industries. But diversification is only one component of GE's smoothly rising earnings, as critical articles in the financial press have noted. Although senior management vigorously denies any nefarious intent, the company has long made a practice of timing asset sales to coincide with restructuring charges. When asset sales produce gains, managers hunt up underperforming assets or business units that would have to be written down anyway. There is no compelling business reason for writing down the assets in one particular quarter rather than another—the timing is determined by the timing of the offsetting asset sale. In addition, the company has been accused of timing the sales of shares in other companies to produce gains when needed. Former chairman Jack Welch has defended the practice—"We're not managing profits, we're managing businesses" is his standard reply. Nonetheless some investors and commentators have come to believe there is a disconnect between GE's smooth earnings and the underlying volatility of its business units.

There are a number of difficulties with the argument that income smoothing is really done for investors' benefit. The first is the contempt for their intelligence implied by the suggestion that investors are incapable of filtering out statistical noise without management's assistance. A second objection is that management's view of the company's future, however well informed it may be, is not infallible. How many senior executives, after all, predicted that the Internet would usher in a new era of explosive profitability at their company? The other problem with management's argument is that smoothly rising earnings are themselves a sign of suspect accounting to seasoned analysts and investors. Instead of suggesting that a company's earnings-generating capacity is stable, smoothed numbers can wind up suggesting the opposite. And finally, how many investors, with the disasters at Enron, WorldCom, and Tyco fresh in their minds, are likely to believe that overprovisioning and other forms of income smoothing are for their benefit?

How Much Is That "Worthless" Inventory Worth?

Write-offs of supposedly obsolete inventory can also be treated like a reserve to provide a handy income boost. The trick is to write off the inventory while it still retains some economic value. In May 2001, Cisco took a staggering $2.25 billion inventory write-off, one of the largest of its kind in corporate history, assuring analysts that the company planned to scrap most of the items in question. But Cisco later rummaged through this scrap heap of "worthless" gear and found some parts worth using. The result was a gain of $290 million from the sale or use of the written-off inventory, helping the company limit its losses in the first quarter of fiscal year 2002. The company would have been content to pass off that gain as the result of improved operations, but under sustained pressure from investors, Cisco did eventually disclose the inventory's effect on profitability. Interestingly, the company initially claimed there was no way to track the inventory once it had been written off—until it came to light that Cisco had segregated the equipment in a separate warehouse.

When confronted with evidence that they have manipulated expense provisions or inventory write-offs to produce the illusion of higher earnings, company managers sometimes respond by saying that the amounts involved, while appearing large in absolute terms, are only modest percentages of total profits, revenue, or whatever accounting measure is at issue. But if the amounts are so small, why does the company bother with them at all? The answer is that though the manipulated figures constitute a small proportion of overall revenue or profits, they often constitute a large percentage of profit or revenue *growth*.

To illustrate, imagine a company that reported profits of $300 million last year. The market expects profits to grow to $330 million in the coming year, a 10 percent improvement. But the company can't meet this expectation, at least not through honest accounting. An honest profit figure might be, say, $315 million, or 5 percent growth. Now imagine that the company reverses $15 million in provisions taken in a previous year, allowing it to reach its $330 million target. Although the reversed provisions amount to only 5 percent of total profits, they account for 50 percent of the profit *growth* in that year. Our example is hypothetical, but plenty of real companies have played similar games to report robust revenue growth.

Comprehensive Income: A Handy Hiding Place

One of the least-tracked areas of the corporate balance sheet is the shareholders' equity section. (One reason it receives so little attention is that transactions in this section have no impact on earnings per share, which is all that most stock analysts care about.) Companies that adhere to the U.S. accounting regime (a category that includes both U.S.-based companies and foreign companies that list their securities on U.S. exchanges) can play all sorts of tricks with a category in the shareholders' equity section known as "comprehensive income." This category is meant to cover a variety of gains or losses that do not figure in net-income calculations because their true impact on earnings is not yet certain, irreversible, or realized. Items that might appear in the comprehensive income statement include unrealized ("paper") gains and losses on investments in financial securities, gains and losses on derivatives transactions used to hedge risks, and gains or losses incurred when translating the financial results of subsidiaries from local currency to the parent company's currency. Management has considerable discretion in determining which gains and losses should be reflected on the income statement and which should be captured in comprehensive income. And by now, it should be clear that where managers have wide discretion, accounting games are sure to follow.

Under U.S. accounting treatment, gains or losses in currency translation must appear in the income statement if a subsidiary's working (or functional) currency is deemed to be the same as the parent's. For example, if the foreign operation of a U.S. multinational does its business in U.S. dollars, gains or losses from currency translation go straight to the income statement. But when the working currency is deemed to be that of the country where the foreign operation resides, gains or losses appear in comprehensive income.

Straightforward, right? Yes—except for one thing: Who determines whether a foreign operation's working currency is the local coin or the U.S. greenback? Management. And managers have significant latitude in deciding which currency is the functional currency. Some of them abuse their discretion in order to park currency-translation losses in the comprehensive-income category, where they can't trouble the earnings-per-share calculation.

Some investors protested that in 2000, Coca-Cola was able to sweep $965 million of currency-translation losses into comprehensive income by asserting that most of its overseas units treated the local currency as their functional currency. Critics of the move note that in the same reporting period, Pepsi charged most of its foreign-exchange losses to earnings, because most Pepsi subsidiaries were deemed to have used dollars as their functional currency. The discussion would be academic except for one thing: An analyst or investor would have a hard time accurately comparing the financial performance of the cola companies without knowing whether their translation losses were posted to the income statement or to comprehensive income.

We won't take sides in this debate—Coca-Cola and Pepsi may both have made the decision best suited to their unique business circumstances. The question is whether Coke's and Pepsi's management and directors should voluntarily disclose what the financial impact would be if their decision had gone the other way. For example, should Coke have mentioned, in the Management's Discussion and Analysis section of its annual report, that it would have reported lower earnings if the dollar had been the functional currency of its foreign operations and currency translation losses had been consequently posted to the income statement?

Recent legislation governing corporate financial reporting, especially the Sarbanes-Oxley Act of 2002, may make such discussion standard, because the law requires management to discuss and explain "critical accounting decisions."

Lucky Guess: How to Turn Pensions into Profits

Corporate pension funds represent one of the most insidious accounting landmines. Because pension accounting is so complex, management has wide latitude to name its own profits. In essence, through much of the 1990s, many companies treated their pension plans as giant cookie jars. Consider a company with an old-fashioned defined-benefit pension plan (that is, a plan that promises pensioners a specific annual benefit; other plans, such as 401(k)s, define not the benefit, but the amount of the employer's and the employee's contributions). The plan holds assets—primarily stocks and bonds, but other financial assets and real estate as well. The assets are supposed to generate income and increase in value over time, providing the funds with which to pay pension benefits to employees when they retire. By law, companies must acknowledge their pension obligations in the footnotes to their financial statements. The footnotes must explicitly compare the value of pension-fund assets against the amount owed.

But there's a twist. Pension accounting involves a series of estimates. Wily managers long ago discovered that they could use their discretion over pension accounting to transform a sizable pension *expense* into pension *income*. No cash changes hands; nothing is produced or sold. Management merely estimates how much its assets will return and then accounts for its pension costs accordingly. Other assumptions, such as the interest rate used to calculate the present value of expected pension benefits, are also subject to managerial discretion. By choosing a higher rate, and thus reducing the present value of future benefits, management can understate the company's pension obligation.

Let's take a closer look at one of the most popular pension games, which uses an overly aggressive estimate of future returns on pension assets. Table 4-1 shows how different return estimates affect the number that appears on a hypothetical corporation's income statement as pension expense (or less often, negative pension expense, or pension income).

Let's define the terms that are found there. First, the *service cost* of a pension plan is the present value of pension benefits earned by employees in the current year. In other words, service cost is equal to the amount pensioners will be paid in the future for this year's service, assuming the money grows at a given rate—the discount rate—for a given period of time.

TABLE 4-1 How different return estimates affect the number that appears on a hypothetical corporation's income statement as pension expense.

Expected Return Rate			
	8%	9%	10%
Service Cost	$25	$25	$25
Interest Cost	$60	$60	$60
Expected Return	$72	$81	$90
Pension Expense (Income)	$13	$4	($5)

Next in the table is *interest cost*. In essence, this is the amount of increase in the present value of prior years' service costs. Because those costs are one year closer to being paid out, their present value increases. The increase is captured as *interest cost*.

Next we have *expected return*. This number is the product of the market value of plan assets (the market value, that is, as of the date of the financial report) multiplied by the expected rate of return on those assets. The rate of return is subject to managerial discretion, although the Securities and Exchange Commission has begun to crack down on overly aggressive estimates. For the purposes of our table, the market value of plan assets is $900.

The final term in our table is the really important one: *pension expense* (or less often, *pension income*). Pension expense is determined by subtracting *expected return* from the sum of *service cost* and *interest cost*. Now we can look at the table and see the effect that different expected returns have on pension expense calculations.

There are a few things worth noting about pension expense or income. First, because such estimates are always highly contingent, we recommend backing pension income out of reported profits. Even companies that report pension expense, as opposed to pension income, however, may be overstating the performance of pension assets—and understating the effect of pension assets on the company's true financial condition. Consider the middle column of the table above. Is it reasonable, in today's investment climate, to expect pension assets to grow at a 9 percent rate? Probably not, given that annual stock-market returns have been negative for three straight years since 2000. So, even if the management of our hypothetical corporation selected a 9 percent expected rate of return, and thus reported a pension expense, that expense, as a measure of future liability, might be significantly understated. As this book went to press, Berkshire Hathaway, superinvestor Warren Buffett's holding company, was using 6.5 percent as its expected return. If the company in our hypothetical example used the same rate, its pension expense would be $26, twice the expense incurred using an assumed return of 8 percent.

Of course, underestimating expected returns will overstate pension costs. But such overstatements are rare. For one thing, they would have a negative effect on current profitability—which is almost always management's first concern. Such overstatements would have a positive effect on profitability in later years, because the differences between actual and expected returns would be gradually used to reduce future pension costs. But, given incentive systems that reward current performance and short-term profitability, management rarely concerns itself with long-term profit strategies.

That view sounds cynical, but it is supported by hard evidence. Millman USA, a benefits consulting firm, estimates that large U.S. companies added a staggering $54.4 billion dollars to their reported 2001 earnings as a result of profits—*assumed* profits—from pension-plan investments. This is an amazing finding, considering that 2001 was a terrible year for the stock market—indeed, the large companies surveyed by Millman suffered collective losses of $35.8 billion on their pension-plan portfolios. Yet even as their plan assets lost billions in value in 2001, corporations made heroic assumptions regarding performance in future years that allowed them to book huge current-year profits anyway. To pick one prominent example, IBM's pension plan lost $2.4 billion in 2001, yet that same year the company reported more than $10 billion in pretax earnings, of which $632 million was attributable to anticipated growth of pension assets. The company assumed, against all available evidence, that pension assets would appreciate by 10 percent annually. But in late 2002, IBM finally acknowledged the unlikelihood of that assumption. It admitted that it might have to contribute as much as $1.5 billion in cash to its pension plan to cover the underfunding caused by the market decline.

Although companies must acknowledge the underperfomance of their pension plans' assets relative to expectations, the difference is reflected in earnings only gradually. To reduce earnings volatility, U.S. accounting conventions permit the underperformance to be amortized over a period equal to the expected service lives of employees covered by the pension plan. The practical effect is that companies can report pension income or artificially low pension expense even when securities markets are delivering low or negative returns. One significant consequence is that a company's pension situation can be far worse than its financial reports would suggest.

IBM is one such company. But there are many others. Standard & Poor's has estimated that, while corporate pension plans in the United States were overfunded by about 7 percent in 2000, they were 6 percent underfunded by the end of the following year. According to Credit Suisse First Boston, the total pension shortfall for the companies that make up the S&P 500 had reached $243 billion by the fall of 2002.

Board members and corporate executives who don't track such matters carefully may find their companies in deep trouble. Indeed, pensions are an especially hazardous accounting landmine, because rosy assumptions about the future can mask chronic deterioration in the financial health of a pension plan. General Motors Corp., for one, faces a staggering bill for the pension and health benefits it owes to retired employees. Under even the most optimistic scenarios, that bill will drain the company's cash flows for years to come. According to some estimates, GM's underfunding may be as much as $29 billion. The underfunding may result in such a large current pension expense that not only will it wipe out most of the company's earnings, it may drain so much cash that it will imperil the company's common-stock dividend. Pension benefits are a ticking time bomb for many companies, especially in the United States, and unsavory accounting practices have worsened the problem by disguising it.

What to Ask: How to Sniff Out Dubious Provisions

To discover whether a company is wandering into one of the minefields discussed in this chapter, consider the following:

Are estimates for uncertain events (such as doubtful accounts and restructuring reserves) included in the financial statements? Has management itemized all provisions and certified that the amounts reported reflect its best efforts at estimating the true costs?

Do the financial statements present a reasonable measure of operating expenses and revenue in the current period? Has the company fully and clearly disclosed the nature of its estimates and how it accounted for them?

Do items in comprehensive income—such as foreign-currency gains and losses and investment gains and losses—actually belong in the current period's net income?

Be wary of large inventory write-offs. By writing off the entire value of inventory while it in fact retains some value, management can create a cookie-jar reserve that is very difficult to track.

Has management taken large write-offs, and if so, is the amount defensible? Board members, investors, analysts, and auditors must be especially wary of management's propensity to take advantage of exceptionally good years, or exceptionally bad ones, to overprovision and create hidden reserves. Are profits and losses in subsequent periods influenced by these write-offs, and is the impact disclosed clearly in the footnotes and management's discussion and analysis? Because provisions can be so hard for outsiders to track, the onus is on insiders—directors, auditors, and finance professionals—to keep management honest. Not only should they insist on reviewing all activity in provisions accounts, they should insist that any reversals of provisions be prominently, clearly, and publicly disclosed.

For each component of provisions, monitor all increases and decreases. Is there any evidence of reversals of provisions from previous years? Be skeptical if the company is reporting higher profits while at the same time showing declining balances in its provisions.

How different would reported earnings be if the method of estimating provisions and unearned income were more conservative, more aggressive, or more consistent with that of key competitors? Are the questions clearly discussed in the Management Discussion and Analysis? If alternative accounting treatments, and their consequences, are not discussed, it could mean the company is trying avoid scrutiny and comparisons with its peer group.

Pay close attention to changes in measurement methods. If a company changes its inventory accounting or its way of measuring receivables or unbilled receivables (in the case of percentage-of-completion contracts), ask what is motivating the change. Likewise, ask why unearned or prepaid income is being transferred from unearned income to revenue. The key questions to ask in the case of any change in measurement methods are these: Why are the changes occurring now—does it help the company make current-year earnings targets? Will hitting those targets trigger bonuses for management?

In the case of global enterprises, watch for a change in the designation of the primary or functional currency of foreign subsidiaries. If they designate their local currency as their functional currency, they may be motivated by a desire to divert translation gains and losses into comprehensive income, the twilight zone of shareholder equity.

Do the changes in measurement methods or reserve balances have the effect of shifting earnings from this year into the future? If management increases its reserves for bad debts, mergers and restructuring, or inventory write-downs, don't automatically assume the company is acting prudently. Management may actually be setting up reserves to supplement future earnings as needed.

Are earnings too strong or too steady? If earnings grow steadily in spite of uneven industry growth, provisions may be smoothing the way. And if reported earnings consistently just meet or slightly beat analyst consensus expectations, look carefully to see if reserves are being trimmed or expanded.

How is the company reacting to changes in customer base, product mix, manufacturing locations, or geographical concentration? Have its provisions changed to reflect changing business conditions and activity?

Are reserves related to acquisitions and sales being used to hide mistakes in previously overstated earnings or to generate artificial future earnings growth through use of merger and discontinued-business reserves?

Is the company's apparent performance being boosted by over-optimistic assumptions about pension-fund returns? Examine the footnotes for management's disclosure about the expected rate of return on plan assets and its effect on current profitability. Does the expected rate of return seem reasonable in the current investing context? Or does it seem unduly optimistic? If it seems unrealistic, try some adjustments of your own. Deduct pension income from reported profits. Don't wait for management to disclose that it will have to commit additional cash to the corporate pension fund: Assume that most corporations with a pension plan will soon be presented with a large, painful bill for their future pension liabilities. Remember: According to Credit Suisse First Boston, the total pension shortfall for the companies that make up the S&P 500 had reached $243 billion by the fall of 2002.

5

A LANDSCAPE OF HAZARD: THE NEW WORLD OF BUSINESS RISK

Risk management has emerged as perhaps the most perplexing issue confronting corporate executives and directors, as well as the investing public, in the new century. Risk is an essential component of business, just as it is of life itself. No value is created without risk: Only by taking risks can enterprises generate growth, embark on acquisitions, develop new products, or establish new industries. But if a company doesn't manage its risk appropriately, the results can be catastrophic. That is why companies expend so much human, intellectual, and financial capital on risk—quantifying it, managing it, disclosing it, analyzing its potential benefits. Risk will probably claim an even greater share of corporate resources—and investors' attention—in the future.

In recent years, entirely new categories of risk have sprung up alongside the hazards that businesses have faced as long as human beings have engaged in commerce. New technologies have sparked a proliferation of novel business models and strategies, each carrying its own risks and possible benefits. The average tenure of CEOs and other top executives has shrunk, increasing the risk of unplanned management discontinuity. The emergence of the information economy has increased the risk of the loss or obsolescence of intellectual capital and proprietary knowledge. Environmental risks may saddle corporations with crushing burdens in the near future. And the risks of terrorism, political turmoil, and war are no longer merely local but global in their scope and potential lethality.

Day to day, though, the greatest risk to business enterprises is the same as it ever was: financial risk, which we define as the risk that a company will become insolvent. At the risk of stating the patently obvious, let us make clear why companies become insolvent: They incur more debt than they can repay. And as we shall see in this chapter, companies often wind up in this situation because they play accounting games that disguise the true extent of their indebtedness.

The consequences of such games can be devastating. Misled about the extent of the financial risk incurred by Adelphia Communications, Enron, and WorldCom, investors poured billions of dollars into those companies' shares and bonds, only to lose it all when the companies collapsed. The damage spread to the accounting firms and investment banks that helped those corporations disguise their debt and borrow still more. But even at companies that manage to skirt bankruptcy, financial risk can exact a heavy toll. People lose their jobs when their employers are hard-pressed to meet their financial obligations. Promising new initiatives go unfunded. Nervous customers withhold orders, deepening the financial distress. Key employees leave, and desirable recruits accept other offers. Long-term planning is slighted as management devotes all its time and attention to crisis management. In sum, excessive, poorly managed financial risk can bleed a company dry. Even if the company survives, financial risk can rob workers of their livelihoods, investors of their savings, and business enterprises of their value-creating potential.

Because financial risk carries so much potential for damage and destruction, it demands prudent management. The first step is clear, full disclosure and quantification of all financial obligations. After all, there is no management without measurement. But measuring indebtedness—and therefore the likelihood that a company will experience financial distress—is far from straightforward. Granted, it is easy enough to track a company's outstanding bonds and bank loans. But other forms of indebtedness are less obvious. In fact, as we have discussed earlier, some forms of debt are not even recorded on a company's financial statements. We have examined how companies hid their liabilities in order to manage their earnings—that is, to manipulate the numbers on their income statements. Now we shift our focus to the balance sheet (and the footnotes to the balance sheet), where risk is supposed to be disclosed, quantified, and discussed, and where it is too often obscured, disguised, and denied. In other words, having scrutinized the income-statement games that corporate managers play with provisions, we will turn our attention to the balance-sheet games they play with debt.

For too long, corporate managers have connived with highly trained, highly paid lawyers, lobbyists, accountants, and investment bankers to shade the truth about the debts incurred by the companies they run. No good has come of these efforts, only a terrible waste of human and economic potential. Financially literate investors, reporters, analysts, and corporate directors must demand that corporations drag all their debt out of the shadows. Until financial risk is reliably and accurately quantified and managed, the next Enron is only a matter of time.

Dark Matter: Where Companies Hide Their Risk

Financial-risk issues can be grouped into three rough categories: off-balance-sheet (OBS) financing, derivatives, and (the accountant's favorite) other. The single biggest hazard facing any corporation—or any of its shareholders, creditors, or employees—is its off-balance-sheet financing. Appropriately, then, our look at risk-related landmines begins with the many clever but ultimately destructive ways that companies shield their indebtedness from the glare of the balance sheet.

Off-balance-sheet financing is a worry point at many companies that otherwise seem to be models of responsible and informative accounting and disclosure. General Electric, for instance, has been a favorite target of critics who contend that the debt of its financial unit, GE Capital, should be recorded as a liability on the balance sheet of the parent corporation. After all, say these critics, if GE Capital failed to honor its obligations, the parent company, GE, would assume the liability, if only to protect its own credit standing. GE expanded its disclosure of GE Capital's debt in its 2001 annual report. But the added discussion didn't satisfy William Gross, manager of the $35 billion Pimco Total Return Bond Fund. In 2002, he questioned the adequacy of these expanded dis-

closures. He contended that GE's voluntary disclosures did not acknowledge the company's dependence on acquisitions to fuel its
earnings growth. He claimed that GE used GE Capital as a cheap source
of financing for those acquisitions and wondered whether a decline in
GE Capital's fortunes would significantly impair the parent company's
ability to continue making the acquisitions that drove the company's
earnings growth. Almost heretically, Gross concluded that GE did not
deserve its blue-chip, AAA bond rating, because it was not adequately
disclosing its risks.

Risk Disclosure: How Do You
Know What You Don't Know?

The issue of GE's debt highlights concerns that corporate managers have too much discretion to decide whether to list certain debts and
obligations as liabilities on the balance sheet. In assessing whether management has abused its discretion, investors, analysts, auditors, and directors should be guided by a series of questions. Has the corporation
incurred debt that is not reflected as a liability on the balance sheet? Is
this debt accurately described in the footnotes to its financial reports? Regardless of the company's own accounting, should its off-balance-sheet
obligations be considered debt when assessing the financial risk it faces?

The answers to these questions often come in shades of gray. If
a business sells its accounts receivable to a factor (a finance company
that buys receivables at a discount from a business and assumes responsibility for collecting them) and it receives cash in payment, it can post
the cash to its balance sheet as an asset—if, that is, the business retains
no residual responsibility for collection of the receivables. If, however,
the factoring agreement requires the business to absorb any bad-debt
losses beyond some agreed-upon threshold, then the business has really
just taken a loan collateralized or secured by the receivables. In such a
case, a fair presentation of the company's finances would reflect the accounts receivable as an asset and record the added cash as another asset
offset by a liability, which should be clearly described on the balance
sheet as "loan payable to factor." As with GE, a crucial question then
arises: Are there assets sufficient to cover the liability? If so, is there a
risk that the assets' values may decline or the liability may grow? At
some future point, could the value of the liability exceed the value of the

asset? If so, are this risk and its potential consequences fully, frankly, and clearly discussed in the company's financial filings?

Worries about the stability of asset values may sound extreme or far-fetched, but they are not. Remember, liabilities—the amounts due to bondholders, banks, or other lenders—are legal obligations that do not evaporate. By contrast, the value of assets such as accounts receivable, oil tankers, or office buildings can evaporate with head-spinning speed. Consider how the swiftly declining value of telecommunications assets has affected the finances not just of telecom companies, but of the banks that financed them, such as J.P. Morgan, and the hardware companies that supplied them, such as Cisco Systems.

Off-Balance-Sheet Financing: It's Not Rocket Science

Although the term "off-balance-sheet financing" conjures up notions of exotic and complicated financial instruments, many everyday transactions, such as the rental or leasing of equipment, are actually forms of off-balance-sheet financing. Suppose that a for-profit hospital needs a blood-gas analyzer, a common and expensive piece of medical equipment. If it wanted to buy the machine outright, the hospital—strapped for cash like most hospitals—would have to borrow to finance the purchase. It would account for the acquisition by capitalizing the machine—that is, posting it as an asset (it would probably make up part of the line for "property, plant, and equipment") and the borrowing as a liability on its balance sheet. But if the hospital rented the machine for two years, the transaction would create, for accounting purposes, no asset or liability beyond the hospital's periodic rental payment, which would show up on the income statement as an ordinary operating expense. Such a rental transaction is known as an *operating lease*. It generally consists of a multiyear commitment to make lease payments in exchange for the use of a piece of equipment. Such commitments are supposed to be disclosed in the footnotes to the financial statements of the enterprise that leases the equipment—in our case, the hospital.

But if the lease actually represents a commitment to rent the equipment for most or all of its useful life, the agreement is classified as a *capital lease* by both U.S. and international accounting regimes. In the eyes of the accounting rulemakers, renting equipment for the duration of its useful life is tantamount to buying it. Indeed, without reading the footnotes in a company's financial filings, you can't distinguish between assets owned outright by the company and assets acquired under capital leases. The accounting for capital leases is therefore indistinguishable from the accounting for an outright purchase financed by debt. In both cases, the asset is added to the balance sheet and the payments due on it—payments that for all intents and purposes constitute debt—are posted as a liability.

Many companies that use a lot of expensive equipment—airlines, for example—acquire much of that equipment through operating leases. By doing so, they keep their financial liabilities for their airplanes off their balance sheets, reducing their apparent indebtedness and improving their return on assets (that is, the ratio of earnings to assets; the smaller the assets, the greater, proportionally, the return). For example, AMR Corp., the parent of American Airlines, has over $7 billion in planes and other equipment acquired under operating leases. The leases are fully disclosed in footnotes to AMR's financial statements, permitting credit rating agencies, lenders, and investors to accurately estimate future claims on the company's cash.

Would that all companies were so forthcoming about their use of off-balance-sheet financing. Let's return to our original example of a company that sold its receivables to a factor. If that business retained residual responsibility for those debts—if for example, it remained liable for every dollar in uncollected debt above $20,000—and did not clearly disclose that responsibility, lenders and investors would likely underestimate the financial risk facing the business.

This example is not purely hypothetical. The sale of receivables, with the selling company retaining liability for some or all of the debt, is quite common. There is a large and active market for so-called securitized debt, which is the generic term for securities backed by credit card receivables, car leases, home mortgages, and similar assets that produce cash flows. If a company is actively engaged in issuing securitized debt, as many companies are, then those with an interest in that company's finances have to ask some crucial questions—and keep asking them until they are answered clearly and definitively.

Do the holders of the debt securities retain related residual claims on the assets of the business? What events, if any, will trigger the company's liability? How would the business be affected if liable for the entire amount of securitized debt? Do assets related to the debt, such as real estate, credit card receivables, or aircraft, exceed the value of the debt?

Could those assets be rapidly liquidated for cash in an emergency? This is a key question: Prior to Enron's demise, Arthur Andersen argued that the company's disclosure of its off-balance-sheet financing was sufficient. Andersen's logic: The special-purpose-entities (SPEs) created by Enron did indeed hold debt for which Enron was ultimately liable. But because the SPEs also held assets sufficient to cover the debt, there was no need to disclose Enron's residual liability. This argument ignores two key points: First, the assets could not be liquidated rapidly in a financial emergency. Second, the value of the assets—mostly Enron stock and other securities—would be certain to decline in a financial emergency, rendering them insufficient to cover the debt.

In recent years, investors have made the unpleasant discovery that many companies do not fully disclose the liabilities they retain when they securitize their assets. In the mid 1990s, Green Tree Financial became the dominant originator of so-called subprime mortgages—that is, residential loans to borrowers considered poor credit risks. Green Tree financed its activities by selling the loans to an SPE, which would convert the loans to securities and resell them to investors. Green Tree then used "gain-on-sale" accounting that allowed it to book expected future profits on the securities as current income. The company adjusted those expected future profits, using assumptions about the rate at which borrowers would prepay loans. It also made assumptions about the number of borrowers that would fail to repay their loans. Year after year, both those assumptions were wrong. In 1998, the company had to restate its results for 1997, reducing assets and net income by $308 million, after previously restating results for 1995 and 1996. The reason: Green Tree had underestimated both the prepayment rate and the default rate on the loans. The company had to reduce the expected profits which it had so confidently booked as current income. Further restatements followed in 2000 and 2001, after Green Tree had been acquired by Conseco. Again, the company had underestimated the default rate. The landmines hidden in Green Tree's SPEs were so damaging that they took down Conseco, which filed for bankruptcy-court protection in late 2002, claiming $52 billion in liabilities.

For those with an interest in Green Tree's finances, the company's sin was not that it made loans to shaky borrowers, or even that it chronically miscalculated how those borrowers would behave. The sin was, rather, the failure to disclose clearly to investors that it remained liable for the loans it had supposedly sold to the SPEs, and what events would trigger the liability. Armed with that information, creditors and equity investors alike could decide for themselves whether the potential return on an investment in Green Tree securities outweighed the risk. Lacking that information, they were unequipped to accurately evaluate the company's risk factors.

It might be argued strongly, based on such an incident, that U.S. accounting authorities should insist that companies incorporate, or consolidate, the liabilities of their SPEs into their accounting statements. UK accounting authorities already have strict rules requiring such consolidation. In the 1980s, in response to a series of scandals in which British companies shuffled debt onto the books of sham corporations, British accounting rules were rewritten to effectively ban off-balance-sheet debt. If a company was liable for the debt of another entity, then that debt ended up on the liable company's balance sheet, even if that company did not own a single share of the entity for whose debt it was liable.

Total disclosure of off-balance-sheet liability would seem to fulfill the overarching purpose of U.S.-style financial accounting, which is to give the public an accurate portrayal of the future claims on a company's cash. Corporate America apparently thinks otherwise. In the late 1990s, when the Financial Accounting Standards Board proposed a rule requiring companies to consolidate the liabilities of their SPEs onto their balance sheets, prominent accounting firms, investment banks, and corporations all weighed in against the proposal. They succeeded in getting the FASB to propose much weaker requirements governing disclosure of SPEs and their attendant liabilities. The business lobby claimed that consolidating the liabilities of SPEs onto the balance sheet of the parent corporation would give investors a distorted picture of corporate liabilities. In many recent cases, however,the disclosure would actually have given investors a more accurate picture of potential future claims on corporate cash.

The response of financial institutions to the FASB's attempts to tighten disclosure requirements was, in a word, scandalous. It is also a useful illustration of what we might call the First Law of Accounting Landmines. That Law holds that the more fiercely institutions oppose a proposed accounting-rule change, the more the proposed rule promotes accurate disclosure. To put it another way, when companies mount a concerted campaign against a proposed accounting-rule change, it's a safe bet they have something to hide that the new rule could uncover.

Some of the most hazardous off-balance-sheet liabilities are those triggered by events that seem highly unlikely. For instance, some Enron bonds were issued on terms that required Enron to repurchase them if the company's debt rating slipped below investment grade. When the bonds were first sold, the possibility that Enron, then a much-admired powerhouse, would fall on such hard times was so remote as to seem almost impossible. As a result, many investors ignored the contingent liability that the buyback provision represented. In this case, at least, Enron's vague and sketchy disclosures were less of a hazard than investors' failure to take those disclosures seriously.

During the boom years of the late 1990s, it seemed that companies like Enron and major telecommunications carriers were unstoppable. The explosive growth in the Internet and wireless communications would fuel unending growth at these New Economy companies. So it seemed a mere formality that when European telecoms used their own shares as currency when acquiring other companies, they often promised to repurchase those shares if their price fell below a certain threshold. Such declines seemed unthinkable when the telecom stocks were hitting new highs almost daily. But in March 2000, when it became clear the telecoms' growth projections were grossly overblown, their share prices began a decline that continued almost unabated into 2003. When the prices fell far enough, landmines detonated at many European telecoms. Stock-repurchase commitments required France Telecom to pay nearly 5 billion euros to Vodafone to buy back stock issued as part of France Telecom's purchase of Orange.

Another sort of stock-repurchase agreement has caused serious financial headaches for companies such as Eli Lilly, Dell Computer, and Electronic Data Systems. Those corporations, like many of their peers, regularly repurchase their shares, in order to issue stock to employees who exercise stock options awarded to them as compensation. During the boom years of the 1990s, when most stock prices were rising strongly, such repurchase programs were a serious drain on corporate resources. In order to control their stock-repurchase costs, many companies contracted with investment banks to buy a fixed amount of their own shares at a fixed price in the future. Such a price was higher than the stock price as of the date of the agreement, but apparently within easy reach, given the upward trend in stock prices prevailing at the time.

In March 2000, for example, when its stock was trading around $70 a share, Eli Lilly contracted with investment banks to buy, by the end of 2003, 4.5 million of its shares at prices ranging from $83 to $100. The deal seemed reasonable when share prices appeared destined to grow to the sky. It appeared much less reasonable in February 2003, with Eli Lilly stock trading around $58. As a consequence of a similar agreement, EDS, the data-processing and systems consulting company, in 2002 lost more than $100 million. EDS's agreements required the company to buy its stock at prices as high as $60 at a time when it was trading in the open market at $17.

Dell, Eli Lilly, and EDS disclosed the existence of the stock-repurchase obligations in the footnotes to their financial filings. But they offered scant discussion of the possible consequences if stock prices fell. In making their risk assessments, the companies, like investors themselves, failed to think through the potential impact of a sharp decline in stock prices.

Buried Lines: How Companies
Take On Debt Without Borrowing

Liabilities and risk can pile up even before a company borrows a penny. Here's how: Many companies maintain lines of credit that they can draw upon as business and economic conditions require. Literally overnight, such lines of credit can add billions of dollars to a company's liabilities. In other words, they constitute a classic contingent liability. Yet many companies do not disclose the existence of such lines of credit—and their potential effect upon the balance sheet—until they actually borrow the money.

This landmine burned Calpine, an energy company, which arranged a $300-million letter of credit with Credit Suisse First Boston in August 2000 but did not disclose it in subsequent financial filings. An analyst from Moody's, a credit rating agency, learned of the letter of credit in the course of a routine review of Calpine's finances. Moody's promptly downgraded Calpine's debt to junk status in late 2001.

An undisclosed contingent liability spelled ruin for Armstrong World Industries, a maker of floor coverings, which in December 2000 filed for Chapter 11 bankruptcy reorganization. The liability was related to $142 million of company bonds sold to Armstrong's employee-stock-ownership program, or ESOP. Under the terms of the borrowing, the company was obliged to repurchase the bonds if its credit rating fell below investment grade. Once again, this was a classic contingent liability, but Armstrong did not disclose it in its financial statements. As a result, the public was unequipped to accurately estimate claims on the company's cash. Knowing nothing of the landmine hidden in Armstrong's accounts, most investors, including the employees whose net worth was tied up in the company's ESOP, were blindsided by the company's bankruptcy.

Other potential liabilities should be considered in evaluating a business's financial risk. These are liabilities that are triggered not by any formal legal agreement, but by an implicit obligation on the part of a business enterprise. Coca-Cola Co., for example, has several affiliates that bottle and distribute their soft drinks in various parts of the world. These affiliates have substantial debt, which Coke does not guarantee. Yet if these affiliates were to encounter serious business problems, Coke would almost certainly bail them out to protect its brand and overseas distribution. Should the affiliates' debt, then, be included when assessing Coke's financial risk? And should Coke's financial reports acknowledge the debt? Perhaps yes. But since the tendency of companies is to underdisclose, we believe investors, analysts, bond rating agencies, and other outsiders should factor that tendency into their calculations of a company's value. Management and directors may find the worst case too horrible to contemplate. Outsiders, even if they hope for the best, can't afford that luxury. When assessing a company's potential liabilities, lenders and equity investors should assume the worst.

Price Insurance: Derivatives Demystified

Derivatives constitute the second broad category of financial-risk factors we will consider in this chapter. Called *derivatives* because they derive their value from other financial instruments or relationships, these complex financial instruments achieved notoriety in the 1990s, after they were famously implicated in the downfall of Barings Bank, the travails of Bankers Trust Company, and the demise of Metallgesellschaft AG. Although derivatives may be better known than they used to be, they are not better understood. They have a bad reputation, typified by the joke that defines derivatives as any investment I lost money on last year. But in fact, the term "derivatives" describes a very specific set of financial instruments and agreements. Properly employed, such instruments can protect against, or (in financial parlance, can hedge) risks related to commodity prices, foreign-exchange fluctuations, and borrowing costs.

Because derivatives can have such a large impact on corporate earnings, insiders and outsiders alike must constantly scrutinize companies that make extensive use of them in the ordinary course of business. And as business grows more global and complex, the range of companies likely to use derivatives grows wider. Any company that transacts business in more than one currency is likely to have substantial risk exposure, as are companies that depend upon a steady supply of raw materials to produce their goods. Any company whose borrowing costs are subject to interest-rate fluctuations is another likely user of derivatives. Thus, derivatives are of concern to almost anyone who invests in public companies, lends them money, or has a fiduciary responsibility to their investors, creditors, or employees.

First let's explain why companies would want to use derivatives in the first place. Imagine you have a large family and a limited income that must be carefully budgeted if the family's basic needs are to be met. Let's imagine further that meat is one of the biggest items in the family food budget. You, as family breadwinner, worry constantly about a rise in meat prices. To buy a little price insurance, you arrange with your local butcher to buy a fixed amount of meat for a fixed price over the coming year. The price is slightly higher than current prices for meat. This additional cost, or premium, is to induce the butcher to shoulder the risk that meat prices may rise sharply in the coming year. For you, it buys peace of mind that you have assured your family of an affordable supply of meat for the year to come. Such contracts are, in fact, a common form of derivative known as *commodity futures contracts*. In exchanges in the United States and around the world, futures contracts are traded for many physical commodities—including metals, foodstuffs, and petroleum.

The principles that apply to the arrangement between our householder and his butcher also govern contracts for the ultimate commodity: money. For example, some futures contracts hedge against fluctuations in the value of a foreign currency. Say you live in the United States and plan to visit Japan in six months. You worry that the Japanese currency, the yen, will by then have become more costly (in other words, you worry that in six months you'll need more dollars to buy the same amount of yen). To protect against that risk, you could buy yen-denominated travelers' checks today. But that would tie your money up for six months. So, instead, you pay a fraction of the value of the travelers' checks to buy a yen futures contract. The seller promises to deliver to you in six months' time a fixed amount of yen at a fixed price. In this fashion, you have locked in the price you will pay for yen in six months, and you need no longer worry about changes in the exchange rate.

You can also enter into a futures contract to sell a foreign currency. Say a leather craftsman in Florence sells leather jackets to a boutique in New York. The craftsman expects to be paid in U.S. dollars in three months' time and plans to convert the dollars to euros as soon as he gets paid. To make sure that his dollars will buy as many euros in three months as they will today—in other words, to hedge against a rise in the value of the euro against the dollar—the craftsman enters into a derivative contract to sell a fixed amount of dollars at a fixed price in three months' time. This allows him to lock in the price of his dollars today. He doesn't have to worry about exchange rates in three month's time, because he knows today the price at which he will sell his dollars when they arrive from the boutique in New York.

When interest rates are rising, homeowners with variable-rate mortgages lie awake nights wondering how much their monthly payments will increase. One way to eliminate that worry is a derivative known as an *interest-rate swap*. A borrower with a fixed-rate obligation swaps places with the holder of a variable-rate obligation. In return for a compensating fee, the holder of the fixed-rate obligation assumes the risk of interest-rate volatility. Meanwhile, the holder of the variable-rate obligation buys the peace of the mind that comes from knowing exactly what the monthly mortgage payment will be. It may be more than what is owed under the variable-rate mortgage, it may be less, but the important gain for the homeowner is *certainty*, which is valuable in itself.

Described in this fashion, derivatives seem like eminently sensible tools for managing risk. But the users of these tools do not always use good sense, as we shall see.

Metallgesellschaft AG was a German industrial conglomerate that came to grief when its use of derivatives backfired, sharply increasing risk instead of limiting it. In 1992, the German company's energy group had entered into contracts, some of them running as long as 10 years, to sell petroleum to industrial customers. In doing so, Metallgesellschaft was taking the risk that oil prices would rise sharply. To hedge against that risk, Metallgesellschaft bought derivatives contracts that would increase in value when oil prices rose. In theory, the increased value of the contracts would offset, at least in part, the higher cost of petroleum.

But Metallgesellschaft did not sufficiently consider what would happen if petroleum prices fell sharply, as they did through most of the 1990s. The misplaced bet cost the company some $1.5 billion and nearly took away its independence. *The Economist* magazine observed at the time: "As Chernobyl was to nuclear power, so Metallgesellschaft has become to financial derivatives."

Inadequate disclosure of derivatives exposure also spelled disaster for Asia Pulp & Paper, a Singapore company whose shares trade in the United States in the form of American Depository Receipts (ADRs). The New Stock Exchange threatened to delist the company after Asia Pulp & Paper disclosed, in 2001, that it had overstated earnings by $220 million from 1997 to 1999. The culprit: two derivatives contracts with DeutscheBank, designed to hedge against exchange-rate fluctuations, that the company failed to disclose. Furious that the company had not told them of this risk factor, U.S. investors dumped Asia Pulp & Paper ADRs, whose price fell from $17 to 12 cents.

Despite such disasters, derivatives remain in wide use, precisely because they can be very valuable tools when properly used and disclosed. But even in the most responsible hands, derivatives can have a substantial impact on a company's income and overall financial soundness. That's why companies must fully disclose their derivatives and the risks they entail. But because companies don't always give the public the data needed to make an informed judgment, it's also essential to know the red flags that signal a possible derivatives-related landmine.

That means knowing that loopholes that unscrupulous corporate managers are likely to exploit. During the late-1990s boom, one favorite loophole involved mark-to-market accounting. That term describes the accounting used by mutual fund companies, brokerage firms, and other companies whose chief assets are investment securities. Those assets are revalued every day to reflect the open-market prices paid for similar assets. Say a stock brokerage firm takes a position in IBM, purchasing one million shares on Monday at a price of $75 per share. The shares, with a total value of $75 million, would be included among the company's assets. Suppose that on Tuesday, IBM announces a big new deal with a customer. Investors respond enthusiastically, and at the close of trading, IBM has climbed $3 to $78. In that case, the brokerage firm would adjust its assets upward by $3 million to reflect the higher market price of its IBM shares. In other words, the brokerage firm has marked its IBM position to market.

Marking to market makes plenty of sense when the asset in question is a stock like IBM—widely traded, with a current price that is easily observed and verified. But what happens when a company's assets and liabilities include financial instruments for which there are no active, organized, regulated markets? Enron, famously, attempted to traffic in such abstract commodities as telecommunications capacity and the weather. The company did in fact engage in transactions to buy or sell these "commodities" and listed the transactions as assets. What's more, Enron claimed to mark them to market, even when there was no market to speak of. Enron's energy traders, for example, determined the price of their more exotic products using computer models that purported to estimate energy prices up to 30 years in the future. But though computers may not lie, Enron's were programmed with assumptions that made the contracts appear extremely valuable. An analysis by Frank Partnoy, a law professor at the University of San Diego, suggests that from 1998 to 2000, Enron manufactured $16 billion in false profits by rigging its mark-to-market calculations.

The Enron case points up the flaws inherent in the use of mark-to-market accounting for derivatives transactions. The first, of course, is that mark-to-market accounting is supposed to be used for assets that are fungible and liquid, and many derivatives contracts are precisely the opposite—unique and illiquid. Worse, the people at Enron who determined the prices to be used when marking derivatives contracts to market were the same people who stood to gain by manipulating those prices. United States accounting authorities now forbid the practice of marking energy derivatives to market. They also require that an independent expert confirm the value placed on all derivatives transactions.

Outside the United States, derivatives reporting is still spotty or, in some cases, nonexistent. A study of 73 big Asian banks found that 85 percent did not disclose foreign-currency gains and losses or their net exposure to currency fluctuations. Two-thirds did not disclose derivative investments.

Where the Wild Things Are: Other Financial-Risk Issues

Besides off-balance-sheet liabilities and derivatives, there are several other ways in which a company may understate or fail to disclose the extent of its liabilities. Consider, for example, companies facing large-scale litigation. Perhaps the plaintiffs are contending that a company's products are shoddily made and dangerous. Perhaps the plaintiffs are suing because the company, they believe, has engaged in widespread, persistent race or gender discrimination. Perhaps they're suing because the company's previous manager failed to adequately disclose the company's liabilities. In any case, has the company fully and fairly disclosed this litigation and its possible impact on company finances?

Halliburton's purchase of Dresser Industries has become controversial because of questions regarding Dresser's disclosure of asbestos-related liabilities. Prior to the acquisition, Dresser executives informed Halliburton that the company faced lawsuits from former employees claiming the company negligently exposed them to asbestos, a known carcinogen. However, the Dresser executives said that they expected to prevail in the lawsuit and that any adverse judgment would not have a material effect on the firm's finances. Famous last words! Dresser's liability for asbestos exposure runs into the billions of dollars, and Halliburton is now busy litigating the question of whether it has inherited Dresser's liabilities.

In contrast to Dresser's failure to inform, consider the exemplary disclosure of Corning, which several years ago faced a sizable claim from women who said they had been injured by silicone breast implants made by a Corning subsidiary. A student of one of the present authors had been offered a job at Corning and was considering whether to accept it. The author urged the student to engage in due diligence and look for disclosure of the liability in the footnotes to the financial statements in Corning's annual report, as well as in the company's proxy statement and 10-K (an expanded version of the annual report, with additional financial information). Corning forthrightly disclosed the litigation and acknowledged that the financial impact on the company could be severe. The report did not offer any dollar estimates for the total cost of the litigation, because doing so would have weakened the company's negotiating position with the plaintiffs. In such a case, disclosure really is a judgment call. Corning management decided, probably rightly, that too-full disclosure was itself an added risk factor. Nonetheless, the disclosures served their purpose: to give people with an interest in the company's financial health—in this case a prospective employee—enough data to make an informed choice.

The High Cost of the Future: Hidden Pension Liabilities

We discussed pension accounting in an earlier chapter. We examine it again here, because no discussion of the risks of hidden liabilities can be complete without including pensions. These, at many companies, impose enormous future obligations that outsiders might not be able to see and that insiders might prefer to keep hidden. As we did earlier, we confine our discussion here to so-called *defined-benefit* pensions, under which a corporation is obliged to pay specified periodic benefits to retired employees or their dependents. The accounting for so-called *defined-contribution* pensions, such as 401(k) plans, is quite straightforward and offers few opportunities for game playing.

Defined benefit pensions, by contrast, are potentially an accounting minefield of enormous proportions. The reason should be familiar by now: An enormous amount of guesswork is involved, and corporate managers have wide latitude to tailor those guesses to suit their own short-term advantage rather than the long-term advantage of the corporation and pensioners they purport to serve.

During the great bull market of the 1990s, companies got used to the idea that ever-increasing stock prices would allow the value of pension-fund assets to easily keep pace with growing pension obligations. But the dot-com meltdown, and the long bear market that followed, have had predictably dire consequences for corporate pension funds. While pension obligations have kept growing in many cases, the value of plan assets have moved in the opposite direction.

At some point, pension funds become so seriously underfunded that companies have no choice but to make large cash contributions. Less cash is then available for investment, debt repayment, and dividends. This is sad news, and what makes it even more distressing is that much of it is kept hidden from investors.

Recent estimates peg the pension-fund shortfall in corporate America to be in the hundreds of billions of dollars, and yet most of these obligations will not be found on corporate balance sheets. The gap at General Motors is so huge, analysts fear, that even if the company's recent operating improvements continue unabated for several years, little cash flow will be left for investors. GM's only hope is a surging bull market that sharply lifts the value of its pension-plan assets. Otherwise, the company will have to find billions in cash to pay off retirees.

Although less extreme than the GM example, many European manufacturers, especially those with large blue-collar workforces, face similar problems. The bond rating of the German steel giant Thyssen-Krupp was recently downgraded, mainly because of concerns over unfunded pensions. Rating agencies put French tire maker Michelin on notice after disclosure that the company had to contribute over 300 million euros to its pension funds in 2002, roughly four times its contribution in the previous year.

Ordinarily, companies have several years to make up the pension shortfalls. But certain events can trigger an immediate demand for a company to make good on its entire pension obligation, once again setting off an unanticipated demand on corporate assets. For example, if a company in the United States shuts down a subsidiary, and that subsidiary maintained its own separate pension plan for its employees, the plan is subject to audit by the federal Pension Benefit Guaranty Corporation (PBGC). If the PBGC determines that the plan is underfunded—that is, its assets cannot be reasonably expected to grow fast or large enough to cover the pension bills likely to come due in future years—the PBGC will demand that the parent company remedy the underfunding immediately. That means the parent of the shuttered subsidiary must immediately contribute cash to the fund sufficient to bring its assets to a level (theoretically) commensurate with all future pension claims. It is the board's responsibility to identify all potential sources of such peremptory claims on corporate cash, and to disclose them on the balance sheet.

As always, we conclude this chapter with some questions readers can ask to help them detect the presence of financial risk management landmines.

The most important question: Are there hidden liabilities that can spark the demand for immediate cash and reduce current or future earnings? Are those liabilities absent from the balance sheet and income statement but disclosed in the footnotes, 10-K and proxy statement, or other official reports to shareholders? Are the disclosures revealing or confusing? Do they allow shareholders to understand the potential costs facing a company? Is the impact of some costs hidden from shareholders? If so, how does management justify hiding those costs? Because shareholders cannot be expected to know what they don't know, it is incumbent upon the board of directors to diligently locate and disclose all potential liabilities, whether or not their disclosure is mandated by accounting rules.

What financial-risk-management programs are in place? Is the company involved in the derivatives markets? If so, what instruments are being used? Are they familiar, and is their behavior predictable, or are they exotic and untested in adverse markets? Are the risks of the company's derivatives positions adequately discussed in management's financial reports? What would be the impact on derivative values and earnings if exchange rates, key commodity prices, and/or interest rates rose or fell by 1 percent? By 2 percent? By 5 percent?

Are there off-balance-sheet financing arrangements that can become obligations of the business? How are such obligations triggered? Has management adequately disclosed the nature of these arrangements, the triggers that convert them to immediate liabilities, and the potential magnitude of those liabilities? What changes in interest rates, prices, or currency exchange rates might prove costly? How costly? Are such risks explained in clear terms in shareholder reports?

Are there other obligations and commitments that can increase the financial obligations of the business and/or impact future operating expenses? What can detonate these added obligations?

For pensions, has management fairly disclosed the justification and impact of the key assumptions that drive pension expense and pension liabilities? Is the justification convincing—can management, the board, and the auditors explain their pension policy decisions to shareholders without torturing logic, plausibility, or common sense?

6

GOODWILL HUNTING: HOW TO TELL HARD ASSETS FROM HOT AIR

Accounting scandals are something of a tradition at AOL. In 1996, well before it acquired Time Warner, AOL got into serious trouble with the U.S. Securities and Exchange Commission for its policy of capitalizing its customer-acquisition costs. In essence, the company accounted for its expenditures on customer acquisition in the same way it accounted for expenditures on fixed assets such as a building or a machine. Instead of listing the cost as an expense, which is immediately netted out of earnings, AOL capitalized its customers—that is, it listed them on its balance sheet as an asset, valued at the cost of acquiring them.

This was an unusual and extremely aggressive accounting choice by AOL management. Accounting principles in the United States allow marketing costs to appear on balance sheets only under rare and highly restrictive conditions. The SEC limits the practice to companies that operate in a stable business environment and that can provide ample evidence that the marketing costs in question can be recovered in the form of future sales. Only then can a company capitalize those costs, amortizing them in future periods. Otherwise, the costs must be written off as incurred. Nearly all companies follow this practice—but not AOL.

Despite the highly volatile nature of the Internet business, the company capitalized deferred membership acquisition costs, amortizing them over the ensuing 24 months. By the middle of 1996, a third of AOL's assets were in the form of capitalized acquisition costs. The total represented more than half of AOL's shareholders' equity. By treating customer acquisition as an asset rather than an expense, AOL transformed a pretax operating loss of $180 million in 1996 into a pretax profit of $65 million—but not for long. The SEC sued AOL over its accounting choices, and the company resolved the dispute by restating its results in November 1996, pushing its stock price below $30, down from a high of more than $60 in April 1996.

The AOL controversy illustrates the two most problematic asset-accounting issues confronting most companies today. First, it highlights the disagreements over what constitutes an asset. Second, it suggests that defining and measuring assets is likely to be even more controversial and uncertain in the future, thanks largely to the increasing economic importance of intangible assets such as knowledge and information.

Assets are generally defined as resources with current or intrinsic value, such as cash, or resources that can be used to generate future revenue, such as a building that is used to manufacture a product or an inventory that will be sold for a profit. Under that definition, AOL argued, the subscription revenue that it would receive from customers was an asset because it constituted a future benefit. AOL further claimed that the costs it capitalized were direct expenditures on subscriber acquisition— the costs of printing, producing, and mailing starter kits to millions of Americans, and the costs of direct-marketing programs such as the response cards inserted in magazines. No indirect or general marketing costs were included. So why did the SEC sue AOL?

First, AOL was operating in anything but a stable business environment. In the 1990s especially, the Internet business sector was characterized by rapid technological change and free-for-all competition. Given the nascent state of the business, and its turbulent customer demographics, AOL could not possibly predict customer retention rates with any accuracy. Nor could it predict the pressure that increasing numbers of rival players would exert on AOL's pricing. Taking those factors into account, the SEC argued, AOL's only acceptable policy was to expense its marketing costs as they were incurred.

The AOL case raises troubling issues for board members, analysts, investors, and others with a stake in financial reporting. The problem is that we are trying to measure digital-age enterprises with accounting systems devised in the analog era. In an economy where information is more valuable than most physical goods, there is legitimate uncertainty about what truly constitutes an "asset" worthy of inclusion on a corporate balance sheet.

The uncertainty is vividly illustrated by the cumulative $160 billion in asset write-downs taken between 2001 and 2003 by AOL Time Warner and two other humbled giants of the so-called New Economy, JDS Uniphase and WorldCom. Those write-downs—by far the largest losses ever to appear on a corporate income statement—demonstrate the difficulty of valuing assets in a rapidly changing business environment. And the losses borne by shareholders of AOL Time Warner, JDS Uniphase, and WorldCom show how costly it can be to get those asset values wrong.

Assets 101: A Primer

Although the basic definition of an asset seems simple enough, accountants have their own way of looking at the world, and it doesn't always correspond with the way the rest of us view things. To capture economic reality in a measurable and observable fashion, accountants rely on filters. In the case of an asset, these filters tell them whether it is worthy of inclusion on the balance sheet and should also give some guidance on how to measure it.

Broadly speaking, a resource must meet three criteria to be designated an asset. First, it must be of future value to the firm. The company should be able to extract some economic benefit from it, either in the form of cash flows if the asset were to be sold, or in the form of revenue generated by the asset's contribution to the firm's operations. For example, a fixed asset such as a stamping machine can be used to produce salable goods. Second, the company must own the item in question, or at the very least have some exclusive ownership privilege. Assets acquired through capital leases meet this criterion, even though legal title does not rest with the company using the asset; the lease gives the company exclusive rights to the asset for the lease period.

Although there are occasional disagreements over the first two criteria—the debate over when a lease must be capitalized is one notable example—most of the controversy in the accounting for assets revolves around the third criterion. Simply put, assets must be measured, quantified, and expressed in some currency (such as the U.S. dollar). No asset can be included in a balance sheet if its value cannot be observed and quantified. But here's where the controversy lies. Not only must the asset be quantifiable, it must be so in a reasonably objective fashion. In other words, an asset cannot be said to be quantifiable unless more than one observer can verify its value.

Verifiability implies that if one financial expert were to value a particular asset for inclusion in the balance sheet, other experts would arrive at a similar value. These valuations don't have to be exactly the same, but they should be close. Verifiability is the basis for effective audits. How is an auditor to sign off on the value of an asset unless it is arrived at by a method that the auditor can observe and confirm?

Try and Catch the Wind: Valuing Intangible Assets

Objectivity was more easily achieved a generation or two ago. In the old days, assets were almost exclusively the physical, bricks-and-mortar kind, the sorts of assets that an auditor can kick, touch, feel, taste. More recently, however, companies have invested increasingly in assets of a more ephemeral nature. Instead of taking physical form—such as machinery, buildings, or equipment—these investments are intangible, taking the form of know-how, intellectual capital, and other assets that don't have physical substance but that may offer the potential of huge future benefits. (Financial assets such as receivables and marketable securities also lack physical substance, but they are considered a separate category, because in most cases their value can be determined with relative ease.) You can't see, kick, touch, feel, or taste intangible assets, but they have economic substance anyway. Because the world's prevailing accounting models are legacies of an earlier economic system dominated by smokestack industries and real, physical assets, however, accounting regulators have struggled mightily with the challenge of how to properly account for intangible assets.

In most countries, only intangibles acquired from outside the firm, in an arms-length transaction, appear on the balance sheet. Acquired intangibles, by definition, come at a price, arrived at in a genuine market transaction, and thus have an objective, verifiable value that the auditors can observe and approve. It doesn't mean that the company paid the right price for the asset, only that the price is observable. It's an objective reality.

Because only externally acquired intangibles appear on the balance sheet, research and development costs are expensed. Ample evidence shows that companies create valuable assets through R&D activities, but the relationship between current expenditure and future benefit is so iffy that the Financial Accounting Standards Board (FASB), chief accounting rules-making body in the United States, decreed in the early 1970s that companies must write off all R&D costs as incurred. Most companies around the world, even those that prepare financial statements using non-U.S. standards, follow a similar practice. Thus, the patents that companies purchase outright appear on balance sheets, since the market transaction establishes a measurable, verifiable value. Patents developed internally through a company's own R&D process, regardless of how valuable they might be, usually do not show up on the balance sheet.

Since the 1970s, the FASB has introduced several nuances to its policy regarding intangibles. For example, in the 1980s, the FASB ruled that software development companies must capitalize and subsequently amortize software development costs beyond the point at which the technological feasibility of the software is established. The practical effect of that ruling is that most companies write off software costs until a workable prototype has been produced; at that point, incremental costs required to further develop the product and ready it for market are recognized as an asset. The logic here is that beyond the prototype stage, the relationship between current cost and future benefits is more certain for software than for other products of the R&D process.

Management determines the point at which software can be capitalized, but the auditors must concur. Once the switch is turned on and the weight of further R&D costs is lifted from the income statement, profits increase as the expenditures accumulate as an asset. When Kendall Square Research, the bankrupt supercomputer company discussed in earlier chapters, needed earnings to demonstrate its profit potential to Wall Street, it began capitalizing software R&D costs. By capitalizing more than $3 million in such costs, KSR was able to report a tiny, $6,000 profit (before restating) in the fourth quarter of 1992. When the company restated earnings, it reversed the 1992 decision to capitalize, suggesting that management could not defend its earlier judgment that the software was past the research phase and that the decision to capitalize was driven mainly by the desire to show a profit to potential investors.

Why have accounting authorities not extended the rules regarding software development to other forms of R&D? Why can't other sorts of product development costs be capitalized? It's an awkward question that has not yet been answered with complete logic and consistency. In some countries—the UK, for example—development costs can be capitalized if several criteria are met, one being a reasonable expectation that related future sales from the products will exceed the capitalized costs. But in most countries, including the United States, all other R&D costs are expensed as incurred, regardless of how promising the resulting technology might be.

In any event, companies have not let a ruling from the FASB deter them from trying to move R&D expenditures off the income statement. Several pharmaceutical companies invest in R&D partnerships and special-purpose entities that keep R&D expenses off their books and spread the risks of new-drug development among several investors. One drug company, Elan, even manages to generate revenue from its R&D partnerships by charging them for services provided and license fees. In 1999 Elan invested $285 million in research entities and extracted $294 million in service charges and license fees from them. In 2000, Elan invested $378 million and recouped $169 million in fees. The practical effect was that the company inflicted less damage on its earnings as a result of R&D expenditure than it would have had it followed more conventional accounting.

Goodwill Accounting: A Study in International Dissonance

The confusion over intangible assets has only been deepened by the FASB's recent pronouncement on goodwill. *Goodwill* is an intangible created when one company acquires another. The acquirer usually pays a price higher than the market value of the acquired company's identifiable assets, such as inventories and equipment, net of any debt taken on. That premium over the net market value of identifiable assets is called goodwill and reflected on the acquirer's books as an asset. In essence, goodwill captures any "unidentifiable assets" bought by the acquirer.

For example, if a company with $1 million of identifiable assets, net of debt, is acquired for $1.25 million, then goodwill of $250,000 is posted as an intangible asset on the acquirer's balance sheet. Theoretically, that $250,000 is the value of the acquired company's name and reputation, as well as its other intangible assets, such as intellectual property and work processes, that cannot be identified and valued separately.

Until recently, U.S. and most international accounting regimes required corporations to amortize goodwill over some maximum time period—40 years in the United States, 20 years in most other places. Amortization charges, though, are an expense, and expenses reduce earnings. For that reason, companies have been no less energetic in attempting to clear their income statements of goodwill charges than they have been in avoiding R&D write-offs. Until recently, many U.S. companies kept goodwill off their balance sheets with the help of *pooling-of-interests accounting*. Called *merger accounting* in some countries, it assumes that the business combination in question is a true merger of equals rather than the acquisition of one company by another. Such combinations must generally be all-stock deals in which no cash changes hands. Otherwise, it is assumed that the company paying the cash must be buying the other—which makes the deal an acquisition, not a merger.

Until the FASB put a halt to it in 2001, pooling was popular among companies because no goodwill was recognized—and consequently there was no goodwill to amortize in postmerger accounting periods. That translated into higher corporate profits. Pooling of interests was especially popular in the late 1990s, as managers, egged on by their investment bankers, used corporate shares, whose prices seemed to rise continually, as currency to acquire other companies. Of course, few business combinations are genuine mergers of equals, and an acquisition is patently not a merger, but if the transaction was structured in the right way with the help of clever investment bankers, lawyers, and accountants, it could still be treated on the books as a pooling of interests.

Companies fiercely resisted the elimination of pooling, because it was one of their most valuable earnings-management tools. The only alternative is to treat each transaction as a purchase, in which one company acquires the other. Where there are purchases, there will also be goodwill. As a sop to corporate America—and with some economic logic—the FASB agreed that while pooling-of-interests had to go, companies would no longer be required to amortize goodwill on a regular basis.

The new pronouncement says that while goodwill must be recognized (assuming the fair value of net assets acquired is greater than the purchase price, which it usually is), companies are no longer required to write it off. Instead, they must subject any acquired goodwill to an annual impairment test. If the goodwill is "impaired"—that is, if its value has declined significantly—it must be written down or written off entirely, with the loss being recognized in that year's income statement. So instead of steady, annual amortization charges, income statements will be charged in an irregular, hard-to-predict fashion.

That's not the only effect of the new rule. Board members and other monitors of financial reporting policies will now have to be even more careful than before in tracking goodwill and in assuring themselves that the balance-sheet values reflect a genuine belief on the part of the company's management and its auditors that there are future economic benefits to be had.

But the new accounting rules have gone further. They now require a higher degree of precision in identifying the intangible assets being acquired. For example, companies must now value "trade dress," which refers to the unique appearance or packaging of a company's products. Well-known examples include the Compaq computer logo, now the property of Hewlett-Packard; the icon, theme music, and promotional slogan of HBO ("it's not TV, it's HBO"), acquired when AOL bought Time Warner; and the Travelers Insurance umbrella that was one of the assets acquired in the Citicorp-Travelers combination. Trade dress can be broadly defined as a product's shape, color, texture, size— indeed, anything that makes it distinctive in the minds of customers.

Prior to the new accounting rules, companies tended to include the value of trade dress in purchased goodwill, which was consequently something of a catch-all account. The new disclosure rules may give investors a more complete picture of what the purchaser actually acquired when it bought the other company—assuming, as always, that management's estimates are made in good faith. Corporate managers might also benefit from being compelled to think with more precision about the assets they are acquiring. As a result, they may be more careful about the price they are willing to pay.

In the coming years, as the trade-dress issue suggests, companies will increasingly be called upon to value more and more assets of a less tangible nature. This is as it should be, because much of what companies invest in these days is intangible. We must admit, though, that when valuing such assets, companies, auditors, analysts, and investors will never have the comfort that comes from observation, as is the case when valuing investments in bricks and mortar or any other tangible asset.

Among the intangibles that corporations will now have to isolate and value are trademarks, patents, and copyrights. The FASB has decreed that such intangibles must be valued in acquisitions separately from purchased goodwill and amortized over their estimated useful life. The intangibles that are amortized will continue to reduce future earnings by an amount that will depend on their valuation and estimated useful life. For example, if a patent is valued at $10 million and is assumed to have a 5-year life, the amortization expense for each of the next 5 years will be $2 million.

Changing any of those assumptions can have large financial effects. Consider what happens when management values the patent at $5 million with a 10-year useful life. In that case the annual amortization expense is only $500,000. The net result of changing the assumptions about this one intangible is an extra $1.5 million in pretax income per year for the next five years. Given the wide array of intangible assets that must now be separately identified, the impact of such choices on corporate earnings can be huge.

In-Process R&D—Managing Earnings with Ideas

Another component of mergers and acquisitions that needs to be valued is something called *in-process R&D*. The term describes the research-and-development knowledge that is included in the purchase price of an acquisition. It is, as you might imagine, very difficult to value such an intangible. Imagine a drug that is in the fifth year of a seven-year trial process. The trials have been successful, but uncertainty remains about future trials and competing drugs. Thus, the research probably has some value, but not as much as a finished, approved drug with an identifiable market and sales history.

In any event, the management of the acquiring company places some value on the drug research, as well as on any other R&D in process at the time of the acquisition. The total value of such R&D is treated as an expense and charged immediately against earnings. Many managers would prefer to take the charge immediately and start the company off with a clean slate, rather than treating the R&D as an asset that will affect earnings until it is fully amortized or written down. Not only does it remove a drag on earnings, it eliminates the possibility that a subsequent large write-off of goodwill will prompt charges that management overpaid. As recently as the late 1990s, it was not uncommon to see 70 percent, 80 percent, or even more of the total purchase price of a target assigned to in-process R&D. Although recent changes in accounting rules, combined with greater scrutiny by SEC staff, have reduced the severity of the problem, in-process R&D write-offs are still fertile ground for serious accounting mischief.

Second-Guessing Management: Auditing Asset Values

The process of valuing intangibles in financial statements is so new that it is difficult to say how reliable it is. But we already see conceptual flaws that could produce knotty reporting problems. We have mentioned that under U.S. rules, goodwill must now be reevaluated annually and any impaired value written down. But we also should point out that if the value of the intangible has increased, no adjustment will be reflected in the financial statements. This is likely to provide fodder for future debates. What we can say at present is that the process will provide much room for judgment; management will be able to defend a wide range of possible asset values. It will be the job of auditors and directors, as well as with investors, to subject management's judgments to rigorous reality-testing.

According to U.S. rules, the work of valuation of intangibles is left to outside consultants, including the Big Four accounting firms (Ernst & Young, Deloitte & Touche, KPMG, and PriceWaterhouseCoopers). The process of valuation varies according to the nature of the intangible. If there is an established market for the asset, valuing it is simple and straightforward. Otherwise, the valuation expert estimates the future cash flows that the asset will generate and calculates the present (or discounted) value of those cash flows.

Of course, it is impossible to estimate precisely how much cash any asset will throw off in the future. But it is possible to determine whether the estimate is reasonable, if management provides adequate information about the factors that fed into its decision making. We already ask management to state its assumptions in valuing pension plans. Isn't it reasonable for directors, analysts, investors, and journalists to insist that management disclose the assumptions behind intangible-asset valuations? It's not an impossible task: Investment bankers already do something similar when valuing a company prior to an acquisition. When management declines to communicate its assumptions clearly, the principle of caveat emptor should apply.

Mark to What Market? Gaming Financial Asset Values

Another example of controversy in asset valuation, resulting from recent developments in financial markets, is the marking to-market of derivatives and other financial instruments. United States accounting rules require companies to mark to market (that is, report values based on prices as of the balance-sheet date) both asset and liability positions in options, futures, and swap markets. In some cases, gains and losses on these positions must be reported on the income statement; for some types of commercial hedging transactions, gains and losses are deferred through the balance sheet account usually known as Other Comprehensive Income.

While there is some controversy over these practices, and abuses of the hedging rule have been noted, at least in these cases readily observable market prices are usually available. But the case of Enron shows what happens when markets are relatively new, markets are not liquid, and verifiable prices are not always available.

Imagine that your company is an energy trader, and that your most important asset positions are in electricity and gas contracts. Until recently, markets for such contracts didn't exist. Indeed, one of Enron's great innovations was to establish such markets. But as the company's collapse has shown, those markets are hardly transparent. If positions are to be marked to market, there must be reliable, verifiable prices. In most derivatives markets, the options and futures contracts that trade there have readily observable market prices. But when trades occur out of the public eye, between, say, a utility and a power broker (such as Enron), how is an auditor to know whether an asset position created by such a contract is properly valued? After all, there is no reference point to tell the auditor whether the prices reported are reasonable or not.

Price-reporting agencies have emerged to fill this gap. Reporters working for these agencies contact the big market participants every working day and ask them what deals were done and at what price. But there's a problem. The reporters are dependent on the good faith of the participants, not just to tell them what deals were struck but also to be honest about prices. In October 2002, both American Electric Power and Dynegy admitted that their traders gave false information to the price-reporting agencies.

Whales and Planes: A Few Old-Economy Tricks

It should be stressed, however, that asset-valuation controversies predate the Internet and the information economy. The depreciation of fixed assets and the accounting for assets acquired through mergers and acquisitions have long been subjects of debate, and these controversies continue. Delta Airlines revised the useful life of aircraft in its fleet twice in ten years; in both cases, the change created sizable increases in reported profits. Were these adjustments motivated by an real change in the airplanes' life spans, by a desire to match competitors' accounting methods, or by some other reason? Nearly always, managers defend such moves either because the change is alleged to better capture the underlying economic reality of the asset's usage, or because the change brings the company more in line with industry practice. Curiously, though, most such changes boost reported earnings.

Some depreciation controversies have their amusing angles. Among the assets Anheuser-Busch acquired when it purchased the Sea World theme park from Harcourt Brace Jovanovich were live sea creatures, including a killer whale named Shamu that was a featured attraction. Harcourt's accountants had treated Shamu as an asset with a constant value that did not need to be decreased over time. Anheuser Busch's accountants disagreed, arguing that even if the creature was legendary, it was not immortal. They came up with an estimate of Shamu's lifespan and arranged for the animal's value to be depreciated over the remainder of that estimated lifespan.

Soft Assets, Hard Questions

What follows are some of the questions board members and other interested parties should be asking managers when evaluating a company's accounting policies for assets.

- *Do tangible and intangible asset values and write-downs of assets reflect real values and changes in value during the current period?* Let common sense be your guide to this question. Consider Tyco's announcement in 2002, amid declining profits and a swooning economy, that it would not write down any of the $26 billion of goodwill on its books. Only one analyst—who in fact had expected Tyco to write down the asset by about 50 percent—expressed surprise at management's inaction. At the very least, management should describe the rationale and key assumptions behind the values it assigns to goodwill and other intangibles. Look for large write-offs of goodwill and other intangibles around the time of an acquisition or restructuring as a means of masking poor investment and management decisions. And during periods of economic distress and reduced profit expectations, management should be required to justify any decision not to write down goodwill and other intangibles.

- *From one year to the next, does the company maintain consistent policies regarding capitalization and expensing?* Be wary of changes, especially of those that result in higher current earnings, such as the decision to capitalize costs that were expensed in previous years. Insiders can test such decisions by comparing capital expenditures with budgeted expenditures. If capital expenditures, as reflected in capitalized balance-sheet totals, exceed the budget, management may be capitalizing operating expenditures to boost earnings. Outsiders will have a difficult time detecting such shifts. If they have any suspicions that management is hiding expenses in capital accounts, they should subject management to aggressive

questioning, voting with their feet if management's
answers are unsatisfactory.

■ *Are the company's capitalization policies aggressive or
conservative?* A policy is said to be aggressive when a
company capitalizes costs that more prudent competitors
would expense. This is particularly relevant to software
companies and to any other enterprise that self-constructs
assets. Managers can abuse their license to capitalize by
adding employee costs and other overhead to asset values, even though those costs are more properly regarded
as operating expenses to be written off as incurred.
Examine capital additions closely: Are property and
equipment really being improved—that is, is their potential for generating revenue truly enhanced? Or are the
"improvements" really just repairs and maintenance—
that is, ordinary expenses? Are capitalized software and
other new-product costs really R&D that should be
expensed?

■ *What is the company's policy regarding underperforming
assets?* Does management delay writing down impaired
assets? Does management write down a wide range of
assets all at once? Such big baths suggests that management is trying to wipe its balance sheet clean of misjudg-
ments and mistakes, especially the mistake of overpaying
for assets. Big baths compromise the consistency and
comparability of a company' financial statements from
one year to the next, and they imply that results were
overstated in the quarters leading up to the write-off.

■ *How does the company deal with doubtful accounts?*
Have adequate provisions been made? Be especially wary
in periods of economic decline or when there is reason to
believe that important customers are encountering financial difficulties. Specifically, what is the allowance for
bad debts as a percent of receivables and how much, as a
percentage of sales, is being written off? Do changes in
these relationships make sense in light of changes in busi-

ness activity, customer profiles, and geographic sources of revenues? Such worries are not merely theoretical: In 2001, Calpine, a fast-growing power producer, was the subject of an unflattering story in the *Wall Street Journal*, which noted that the company had not bothered to establish any reserves to account for potential bad debts when its largest customer, Pacific Gas & Electric, filed for protection from its creditors. Where was Calpine's board while all this was going on? In 2003 Sears, the large American retailer, was embarrassed by unexpectedly high bad debts from its credit card sales, with predictably negative consequences for its shareholders.

■ *Are value adjustments fully disclosed?* For example, if assets have been written off, are there sufficient disclosures to allow an informed reader of the financial statements to understand what assets were affected, in what amounts, and why?

■ *Are the company's asset-accounting practices consistent with industry practices and those of global competitors?* If not, are the differences justifiable and adequately discussed in the financial statements? Before concluding that a company is more or less profitable when compared to prior periods or to its competitors, consider whether past asset-valuation judgments artificially augment current earnings.

■ *Are asset depreciation and amortization policies being used to manage earnings?* Does management maximize current earnings by consistently adopting longer depreciation and amortization periods than those used by the competition? Alternatively, has management adopted aggressive amortization and depreciation policies to generate hidden reserves that can later be realized as gains on asset sales? Carefully analyze all financial-statement footnotes regarding depreciation.

Keep a close eye on the company's largest asset accounts. Is it possible that management is accelerating or deferring earnings by playing with asset values? Firms with large inventories can use those assets to manage earnings. Firms with lean inventories may need to play with the value of fixed assets such as airplanes and factories. Firms without fixed assets or inventories may seek earnings-management opportunities in their intangible-asset values. Remember, the largest asset account is the one most ripe for manipulation. Focus your questions accordingly.

7

The (Inner) Circle Game: Ripping Off Shareholders with Related-Party Transactions

$\mathbf{I}$t's a frustrating thing about accounting: Rules and principles that sound simple and straightforward when expressed are anything but simple and straightforward when applied. Consider the rules governing the disclosure of related-party transactions.

The term "related parties" can theoretically be used to describe anyone or anything that has a preexisting relationship with a corporation. The category includes corporate officers, directors, and other employees, as well as their spouses and family members. It also includes a corporation's creditors and suppliers, as well as entities controlled by a corporation or entities that control a corporation. By virtue of their relationship, related parties can do deals with the corporation on terms that would be unavailable to an independent, unrelated third party. (Deals with independent third parties are referred to as "arm's-length" transactions.)

The transactions are as varied as commerce itself. Related-party transactions (called RPTs for short) might consist of deals between management and the company or one of its subsidiaries—a loan to the CEO, perhaps, or an office-cleaning contract with a corporate officer who runs a maintenance service on the side. A contract with a board member's consulting firm is an RPT, as is an agreement to pay certain living expenses of a retired executive. Buying a wide-screen television for a vendor who gives the company a price break on office supplies is probably an RPT. And it's probably an RPT when a vendor picks up the check for the vacation of the purchasing manager of a corporate customer.

Should corporate officers, boards, and auditors disclose all such transactions—or only those of material significance? Full disclosure seems like a worthy aim, but true full disclosure would deluge readers with minutiae. (Of course, blinding the reader with a blizzard of detail can be a handy strategy if you have something to hide. As we shall see, Enron disclosed its special-purpose entities and even acknowledged that some of them were managed by a senior Enron executive, but it scattered its disclosures across several different filings and shrouded them in dense, opaque language.) But what constitutes materiality? Should a company omit mention of a potentially significant transaction or event, simply because it's trivial in absolute dollar terms? In one recent case, a company's outside auditors did not disclose their finding that management had engaged in a fraudulent transaction. The auditors' reasoning: The amount of the fraud was immaterial in comparison to the company's sales and earnings. But size isn't everything: If a company's officers are willing to engage in fraud, isn't that material, regardless of the size of the scam? If you were a potential investor in that company, wouldn't you want to know that its officers were capable of fraud? More to the point, if you were auditing a company, wouldn't management's willingness to commit fraud raise the suspicion that senior executives might be willing to falsify the company's accounting as well?

Recognizing the risk that RPTs can be abused to benefit a favored few at the expense of the mass of investors and employees, financial regulators in the United States and elsewhere have established rules that are supposed to enable the public to judge for themselves the propriety and advisability of related-party transactions. Those rules, at least as they apply in the United States, are summarized in a bulletin from the American Institute of Certified Public Accountants, which helps set performance standards for the profession. "Related-party transactions," says the bulletin, "should be identified and the amounts stated on the face of the balance sheet, income statement, or statement of cash flows." A memo from the Financial Accounting Standards Board expands on this requirement. Corporate financial reports should include a "description of the transactions and such other information deemed necessary to an understanding of the effects of the transactions on the financial statements." The detailed description of the transactions is necessary, says the FASB, because "transactions involving related parties cannot be presumed to be carried out on an arm's-length basis."

Those instructions, and the rationale underlying them, seem plain and simple enough. Yet few areas of accounting are as ambiguous, as fraught with conflicting definitions and interpretations, as RPTs. One company's arm's-length deal is another company's related-party exchange. The ambiguity is not the result of inadequate guidance on the subject. The official literature on RPTs is voluminous, with page after page devoted to lists of persons and entities that might be considered related parties, as well as descriptions of what might be considered related-party transactions. In both cases, though, the operative word is "might." As careful as the accounting authorities are to define related-party transactions, their definitions are as notable for what they leave out as well as what they include.

To get a sense of the ambiguity around RPTs, consider the controversy over a deal that AOL did with Bertlesmann. In 2000, prior to its acquisition of Time Warner, AOL paid $6.7 billion for 50 percent of Bertelsmann's stake in AOL Europe. About $400 million of that purchase price found its way back to AOL in the form of advertising on AOL purchased by various Bertelsmann units, according to federal investigators. The federal authorities think AOL should have accounted for that $400 million as a reduction in purchase price, not as advertising revenue. But more to the point of our discussion is another question: Should AOL have disclosed the deal as a related-party transaction? After all, Bertelsmann and AOL were partners in AOL Europe. What's more, the very fact that they were seller and buyer, respectively, of a piece of AOL Europe could be viewed as evidence of a preexisting relationship between Bertelsmann and AOL, at least with respect to any deals that emerged from the sale of AOL Europe. Was Bertelsmann's purchase of AOL advertising time a related-party transaction? Ask ten accountants, and you'll probably get ten different answers.

Another set of ambiguous transactions occurred at Cisco Systems. In 2000, a front-page article in the *Wall Street Journal* described a civil lawsuit that accused two Cisco Systems sales executives of extorting stock options and cash payments from a customer. (Cisco subsequently filed a related arbitration claim against the two.) The salesmen defended their conduct by saying that they were merely emulating senior Cisco executives, many of whom invested in technology startups that then became suppliers to Cisco, customers, or both. Although the company insists that there was a sharp distinction between the alleged extortion by the two salesmen and the legitimate investments of its senior executives, the fact is, all the companies that sold early-stage equity to Cisco employees or awarded them options did so to forge closer ties to the company. When is it legitimate to cement a corporate relationship by enriching individual executives? Again, different accountants will offer different answers. So will different shareholders.

Compounding the definition difficulty is a phenomenon that the AICPA describes, with some delicacy, thus: "A common observation regarding related parties is that companies fail to satisfactorily describe the nature of related-party relationships and transactions...." This observation helps explain why any sane investor regards related-party transactions with something approaching alarm. Not only does every company have its own definition of RPTs, few companies assign clear responsibility for capturing, assessing, and reporting them. At some companies RPTs are the responsibility of the CFO; at others, of the board's audit committee. Others operate on little more than the vague hope that *someone* will catch every RPT of material importance. As a result, corporate reports of RPTs tend to be spotty, unreliable, and often useless for purposes of comparison among companies.

The increasingly global nature of business makes related-party transactions even more of a Bermuda triangle. Not only does every company have its idiosyncratic definition of RPTs, so does every country and legal system in which a company operates. In many places, RPTs are an integral part of the culture, and not to engage in them is discourteous. Thus, as an accounting professor in India told one of the authors, the real problem in his country is to identify transactions with *un*related parties. Learning how RPTs are viewed, accounted for, and audited throughout the world is not easy or quick work. But it may be the key to financial survival for companies that do business on a global basis, and for those who invest in, audit, or analyze such companies.

When it comes to RPTs, corporate outsiders—investors, analysts, rating agencies, journalists—are uncomfortably dependent on a company's board, management, and auditors. Responsible companies will systematically define the RPTs that need to be captured in a company's financial reports, develop methods to capture them, and make senior personnel responsible for capturing RPTs and disclosing all relevant details about them. But, of course, that only begs the question: How can outsiders be sure that a given company is one of the responsible ones? How can they be sure the company is reporting every material RPT? More to the point, how can outsiders know what a company is NOT reporting? How can they know what they don't know?

There are no easy, foolproof answers to those questions. The only answer, and it is painfully incomplete, is that outsiders must keep up the pressure and scrutiny. Just as political tyrants refrain from committing human rights violations when they know the eyes of the world are upon them, so corporate managers will hesitate to engage in self-dealing if they know their every move is being watched by skeptical analysts, journalists, and investors.

Many Shapes and Sizes: Varieties of Related-Party Transactions

There are as many motives for disguising RPTs as there are transactions themselves, and we will not attempt to catalog every motive or transaction. But to give you a sense of their range, we will look at some of the most notorious RPTs of recent years, before we conclude with a list of key questions for management.

One of the greatest hazards of RPTs is that they offer numerous opportunities for insiders to enrich themselves at the expense of investors, customers, and employees. The risk is highest when a corporation is dominated by a single shareholder or group of shareholders. Case in point: Adelphia Communications, the sixth-largest cable-television company in the United States, was founded and controlled by John Rigas and his family. In July 2002, Rigas, his sons Timothy and Michael, and two other Adelphia executives were arrested and charged with systematically looting the company of millions of dollars.

In plain terms, the Rigases allegedly treated the company like an ATM. According to the federal indictment brought against them, they used company jets to ferry them to an African safari, spent more than $12 million of company funds to construct a golf course, and borrowed billions of dollars from the company, at extremely lenient terms, for their own personal business ventures. Most pertinently, the Rigases borrowed $400 million to buy Adelphia stock. The family had trumpeted the stock purchases in March 2002, claiming that they demonstrated faith in the company's prospects. But the Rigases came by their faith cheaply, allegedly borrowing the funds for the stock purchase from Adelphia and creating false receipts to make it appear that they had paid for the stock out of their own funds. In addition, the indictment charged that the Rigases used double books to hide their personal transactions and hijacked the company's cash-management system, which commingled cash from Adelphia and the Rigases' private ventures. In short, the Rigases treated Adelphia as if it were still the family's private operation and not a publicly held company with thousands of shareholders.

Such conduct is not all that rare at companies controlled by a single person or entity, although the Rigases' alleged looting was unusually extensive. Such companies require extremely rigorous governance mechanisms if they want to avoid RPT scandals. A substantial number of directors should have no ties to the corporation except for their board memberships. "Substantial" is a term difficult to define with scientific precision, but we would say in most cases it means at least two-thirds of the board. All materially significant RPTs should be approved in advance by a committee of independent directors. Independent directors should also be responsible for capturing, assessing and reporting all related-party transactions. Their definition of materiality should be conditioned not only by the dollar amount of a particular transaction but also by how every transaction reflects on the integrity of management.

The Ties That Blind: HealthSouth, Tyco, and RPTs

Corporate outsiders should be especially wary of related-party transactions involving corporate directors. Such RPTs are a useful way to link directors to the CEO rather than shareholders, and thus are detrimental to good government. Richard Scrushy, the former CEO of HealthSouth, has been accused of masterminding an accounting fraud scheme that lasted from 1986 until it was revealed in 2003. Several members of the board had extensive dealings with Scrushy outside of HealthSouth. For example, venture capitalist Charles W. Newhall III, a member of the HealthSouth board since 1985, was also a director of company called MedCenterDirect, a hospital-supply management company that numbered Scrushy and Newhall's venture capital firm among its investors. Another MedCenterDirect investor was Acacia Venture Partners, a venture capital firm whose founder and chief executive is HealthSouth director C. Sage Givens. Givens and Newhall purchased a medical staffing company from HealthSouth in 1998. Such ties are not in themselves indicators of wrongdoing, but it's reasonable to wonder if the directors' ties to Scrushy blinded them to the fraud that was being carried out on their watch. (RPTs are especially powerful tools in the hands of a charismatic executive like Scrushy. One prominent public figure who was asked—and declined—to join HealthSouth's board described the CEO as "a combination of Elvis and Elmer Gantry. Richard Scrushy *was* HealthSouth.")

Tyco under its former chairman Dennis Koslowski was a classic example of a company that used RPTs to create a culture of shared benefits—and shared secrets. Like the Rigases, Koslowski blurred the boundary between corporate and personal spending, lavishing millions of dollar's of Tyco's cash on a palatial Manhattan apartment whose entryway notoriously featured a $16,000 umbrella stand shaped like a poodle. The apartment was carried on Tyco's books as a property for corporate use, but in fact it was Koslowski's private residence. The former CEO also used RPTs to silence anyone who might protest such misuses of corporate assets. He allegedly gave Tyco general counsel Mark Belnick a $20 million bonus as a reward for approving an even larger bonus that Koslowski gave himself. As this book went to press, both Koslowski and Belnick were under federal indictment for a range of Tyco-related offenses, including larceny, tax evasion, and falsification of documents. Lawyers for both men have asserted their innocence of the charges.

The Custom of the Country: RPTs Overseas

Related-party transactions are also a convenient means of producing the illusion of rapid corporate growth. They're even more convenient when the transactions occur in an environment where lax financial controls are the norm. Many Asian countries have long been tolerant of fast-and-loose accounting, especially as regards related-party transactions, which are integral to the business culture in much of the region. So it is not surprising that when senior managers of Lernout & Hauspie, the now-vanished maker of voice-recognition software, wanted to show rapid growth, they use related-party transactions in Asia to turn the trick.

Lernout & Hauspie's 1999 financial results were a source of great excitement to many investors, in particular many Belgian investors, who considered the company a herald of Belgium's high-tech future and a great source of national pride. The company reported eye-popping growth in 1999, especially in Asia and most especially in Singapore, where sales jumped to $80.3 million in 1999 from $29,000 the previous year. The primary source of that additional revenue: 19 Singapore-based startups—startups launched by Lernout & Hauspie and financed by a venture capital fund whose investors included Jozef Lernout and Pol Hauspie themselves. Those 19 startups—L&H's best customers in the region, remember—had no revenue. Several claimed offices at the same address.

The signs of trouble were there for anyone willing to see them—and that category should have included KPMG, L&H's outside audit firm. The burst of growth was too dramatic to take on faith, especially given L&H's ties to the customers that were fueling the company's growth. Nonetheless, KPMG gave the company a clean bill of health. Relying on that assurance, many investors committed funds to Lernout & Hauspie, only to lose them all when the deception was exposed and the company collapsed.

The Lernout & Hauspie scandal has been described as Belgium's Enron, but in fact the two cases were quite different. After its early innovations in energy markets, Enron increasingly became something of a Potemkin company, an assemblage of shams designed to convey the illusion of genuine commercial activity. Its demise did nothing to hamper innovation—except perhaps the innovation of new accounting games. L&H, on the other hand, was a pioneer of promising voice-recognition technology. Even had the company eventually been split up or acquired, its technology probably would have generated significant shareholder returns eventually. And had investors been able to recognize the company's actual growth potential—which was obviously less dazzling than it appeared—they might have given the company less capital to burn and kept management on a tighter rein. The company's downfall not only slowed the development of voice-recognition software, it demoralized the entire Belgian business community, to whom L&H's collapse was as much a personal betrayal as a financial loss.

Hide in Plain Sight: The Enron Solution

No discussion of RPTs would be complete without a mention of Enron's adventures with special-purpose entities (or Variable Interest Entities, in the terminology of the Financial Accounting Standards Board), which eventually brought the company down. As we described in Chapter 5, many companies use special-purpose entities (SPEs) to isolate—or, on occasion, to hide—risk. Consider Vivendi Entertainment, part of the troubled Vivendi Universal media and entertainment conglomerate. For some years, Vivendi Entertainment (VE) has used SPEs to hold receivables representing fees from subscribers to VE's Canal+ cable-TV unit. Those receivables are then securitized and sold to investors. In effect, Canal+ uses the receivables as collateral for a short-term borrowing. But by transferring the receivables to a separate legal entity (instead of just selling or factoring them outright), VE shields the accounts receivable from claims by Vivendi's other creditors. The result is that the debt raised through the SPE (which is backed up by the receivables) is far less risky to lenders than other loans that might be made to Vivendi. Lower risk translates to lower borrowing costs.

Enron's use of SPEs cannot be so easily justified. There is little point in delving too deeply into the mechanics of Enron's exploitation of loopholes in the rules governing SPEs, since many of those rules have been changed in the wake of Enron's collapse. (Those seeking more detail can consult the *Report of Investigation by the Special Investigative Committee of the Board of Directors of Enron Corp.—February 1, 2002*, better known as the Powers report. It is available online in PDF form at news.findlaw.com/hdocs/docs/ enron/specinv020102rpt1.pdf.) But it's worth pausing to note some of the techniques Enron used to obscure the true nature of its RPTs. Aware of being the center of scrutiny, companies are carefully avoiding the shell-game disclosures that were an Enron trademark. But when the boom times return, another band of clever, unscrupulous operators may use similar techniques to hide their scams in plain sight. In such a case, it may be helpful to refer back to Enron's maneuvers.

The 2000 Enron annual report contains the following statement in a footnote: "In 2000 and 1999, Enron entered into transactions with limited partnerships (the Related Party) whose general partner's managing member is a senior officer of Enron. The limited partners of the Related Party are unrelated to Enron. Management believes that the terms of the transactions with the Related Party were reasonable compared to those which could have been negotiated with unrelated third parties." That is the sole mention of RPTs in the annual report, which for many of Enron's investors and analysts was the sole source of detailed financial information. A diligent financial sleuth, however, could have found another clue about RPTs in the expanded annual report known as the 10-K, which every public U.S. company is required to file. About 50 pages into Enron's 220-page 10-K, there is a brief mention of RPTs that does little more than refer the reader to Enron's proxy statement.

The payoff finally arrives 30 pages into that proxy statement: a wad of financial verbiage that refers specifically to Enron CFO Andrew Fastow and his role as the managing member of the general partner of the LJM2 partnership with which Enron has concluded several transactions. (Partnerships within partnerships are a common structural feature of SPEs, again raising the point that complicated ownership structures are themselves a sign that trouble may lurk in a company's accounts.) The proxy also states that the general partner is "entitled to receive a percentage of the profits of LJM2 in excess of the general partner's portion of the total capital contributed to LJM2...." On the face of it, Enron's disclosure is reasonably forthcoming, but it raises as many questions as it answers. Why did this more specific disclosure appear in the proxy statement but not the annual report? Is it because investors are more likely to study the annual report than the proxy statement, which is stuffed with information but expressed in a manner that only the sleep-deprived could love? And why did neither disclosure accompany Enron's earnings releases, which were the Enron financial filing most widely reported in the media? And finally, should a senior officer of Enron have been entitled to profit from the SPE's transactions with Enron? As de facto manager of the SPE, wasn't he negotiating against himself, or at least his employer?

Of course, none of Enron's disclosures mentioned that LJM2 was in violation of accounting rules governing the level of outside ownership required to keep an SPE off the books of the corporation that set it up. When that violation was discovered, LJM2's finances were consolidated into Enron's accounts. LJM2's liabilities wiped out $1.2 billion of Enron's net worth, which immediately put most of Enron's debt into technical default. The company's sources of finance dried up, putting it out of business almost immediately.

Arthur Andersen, Enron's auditor, pointed to the company's deceptions about the ownership of LJM2 and tried to portray itself as a victim, making the now-familiar excuse that auditors rely on their client's good faith and can't be expected to catch managers bent on committing fraud. While AA was still in business and fighting for its life, partners of the firm made the rounds of colleges and business schools, using annotated copies of Enron's financial filings to demonstrate that Enron's disclosures were adequate and that AA had conducted its audits responsibly. But the AA partners could never convincingly explain how an entity under supposedly independent management came to be directed by a senior Enron executive. Nor could they explain why they did not insist that Enron disclose that Fastow netted more than $30 million as LJM2 managing general partner. And AA was unable to explain how deals so favorable to Fastow could conceivably be equivalent to an arm's-length transaction.

Partly as a result of AA's dereliction in the Enron case, audit firms have lost the trust of the public. And with good reason, we would argue, since audit firms in recent years have shown themselves to be far more protective of their revenue streams than of the public interest. The decline in trust of auditors has impelled many investors to act, in effect, as their own auditors. This can be a difficult undertaking when RPTs are involved, since most RPTs happen out of public view. But accounting landmines are rarely in full view, and their presence must usually be inferred from other evidence. That is why auditors arm themselves with a whole checklist of transactions, prepared by the AICPA, when they start to investigate RPTs. Investors, and corporate outsiders in general, should use the same checklist when they begin their own investigations.

Investors as Auditors: A Checklist for Beginners

Some of the transactions on the checklist are merely questionable and require further investigation before their legitimacy or illegitimacy can be determined. Others are clear evidence of a conflict and must be defended by management. If management's defense is unsatisfactory, the auditor must note the exception in its report to shareholders. Of course, if the shareholder is the (unofficial) auditor, the best way to note the exception may be to sell the stock. In any case, when examining RPTs, watch for:

- Borrowing or lending on an interest-free basis or at a rate significantly above or below prevailing market rates
- Real estate sales at prices that differ significantly from the appraised value of the properties
- Nonmonetary exchanges of property for similar property
- Loans with no due dates or formal repayment terms
- Sales with a commitment to repurchase that, if known, would preclude recognition of all or part of the revenue
- Accruing interest at above-market rates on loans
- Loans to parties that do not possess the ability to repay
- Advances of company funds that are subsequently transferred to a debtor and used to repay what would otherwise be an uncollectible loan or receivable
- Services or goods purchased from a party at little or no cost to the entity
- Loans advanced ostensibly for a valid business purpose and later written off as uncollectible
- Payments for services never rendered or at inflated prices
- Sales at below market rates to an unnecessary "middle man" related party, who in turn sells to the ultimate customer at a higher price, with the related party retaining the difference
- Purchases of assets at prices in excess of fair market value

Of course, outsiders will not even know of the existence of such transactions without the cooperation of management—or perhaps without the assistance of employees who reveal details of the transactions to reporters, analysts, or investors (especially short sellers, who seek to profit when a stock's price declines). Such "moles" or whistleblowers are often reviled by businesspeople, who accuse them of disloyalty. But employees who risk their jobs to inform the public of management's dubious or downright unethical behavior may be demonstrating a higher loyalty—to shareholders, and to the truth.

Whatever their motivation, whistleblowers are valuable if only because they remind management of the first and most important test of any related-party transaction. This test isn't found in any AICPA workbook or FASB bulletin. It consists of one simple question: Would this transaction embarrass the company if its details were published on the front page of the *Wall Street Journal* or the *Financial Times*? If heeded, that question would keep many companies out of trouble, many managers in their jobs, and many shareholders on board. General Electric, for instance, could have avoided at least one firestorm if it had applied the front-page test to its agreement to provide its retired chairman, Jack Welch, with an array of lifetime benefits, including wine, meals, security services, tickets to sporting events, and even toiletries.

Of course, there are many other questions for management and the board to ask—and for investors and analysts to ask of management and the board. The first is obvious: Are all significant related-party transactions and commitments disclosed? From that beginning flows a whole host of inquiries:

Is it appropriate for the corporation to engage in this transaction?

What policy determines which transactions will be disclosed? Does that policy specify the level of detail to be included in the financial statements?

How are related parties defined? Is this definition included in the company's public filings? If not, why not? Which employees, executives, directors, family members, and affiliates are included? Which are excluded? Why? Does the definition of related parties extend to relationships with professional firms such as auditors, investment bankers, and legal counsel? Which transactions with lenders, suppliers, and customers are considered RPTs?

How is materiality defined? Is it determined strictly by a numerical test, or does the definition include ethical, legal, and moral dimensions? How large must the potential impact on the financial health of the company be before it is disclosed?

Are there conflicts of interest that could damage or benefit groups of shareholders? Should those conflicts be disclosed? If not, why not?

Is the disclosure adequate for shareholders and other parties who will rely on the financial reports?

Are all financial reports consistent in their descriptions of RPTs? Are discussions of related-party transactions adequately cross-referenced among the company's financial filings?

Are formal governance procedures in place for dealing with RTPs? How are responsibilities for RPTs allocated among the compensation committee, the audit committee, the full board, management, and the outside auditor? Is the compensation committee kept apprised of related-party transactions? Does it analyze such transactions that involve senior management?

How does the company define independence as it applies to board members? Does that definition afford genuine protection to shareholders?

To what extent do the auditors confirm the related-party transaction data? What tests were done by management and auditors to ensure that the transactions were arms-length or equivalent in value to independent transactions that would be negotiated with unrelated third parties?

If a transaction is questionable or potentially embarrassing, should the corporation disclose it, or would it be more appropriate to simply discontinue it?

Of course, if more corporate managers and directors asked that last question, there would be no need for books like this one.

8

THE MISMEASURE OF BUSINESS: PERFORMANCE COMPARISONS AND BENCHMARKS

Imagine you're a fan of the New York Yankees. During baseball season you regularly check the sports reports to learn how your team fared the day before. One morning you check the score of the previous night's game, and you see the Yankees scored four runs. But a printer's error prevents you from learning how many runs the Yankees' opponents scored. If they scored two runs, great—the good guys won. If the other guys scored seven, well, the Yanks will get 'em next time. But until you know how the opponents fared, you simply don't know whether the Yankees won or lost.

The baseball fan in our example shares the plight of any student of corporate performance who lacks or doesn't know how to use the tools of comparison, which financial professionals call *benchmarks*. Without the means to measure a company against competing outfits, it's impossible to know the score. You may know that a particular company earned $1 per share in the first quarter, but you cannot tell whether that company is outperforming, underperforming, or keeping pace with its rivals, unless you also know what competing companies earned in the same period, and how much revenue or capital they required to produce those earnings. There is no way to assess performance without performance benchmarks.

Benchmarks supply the context that allows managers, investors, auditors, and analysts to assess a company's performance by comparison to a variety of reference points: the company's own performance in earlier periods; its own expectations or those of investors and analysts; other business enterprises; and, above all, its immediate competitors. By assembling a variety of benchmarks into a kind of mosaic, managers, directors, auditors, analysts, investors, and reporters can gain a big-picture sense not only of a particular enterprise, but of the industry it is part of and the larger economy it is situated in. Assembled and analyzed with experience and judgment, benchmarks enable the business observer to see both the forest and the trees. Like most methods of measuring business activity, however, benchmarks allow managers wide scope for deception and misdirection.

Benchmarks are vulnerable to managerial manipulation because business is not like baseball, which has a single standard for keeping score. While every sort of business enterprise needs to keep track of certain basics—sales, expenses, profits, cash on hand—there are as many variations on business scorekeeping as there are companies. Managers are free, within broad boundaries, to pick and choose among the inputs used to calculate their score, and they often tweak those inputs to show their companies in the best possible light. This is to be expected and in fact may be management's obligation: Proper regard for the concerns of current shareholders, after all, requires managers to obtain capital at the lowest possible cost, and flattering performance comparisons can convince investors to pay more favorable prices (favorable from the company's standpoint) for a company's equity or debt. But many performance comparisons cross the line from flattery to outright deception. And even when management does not set out to deceive, the various accounting systems in use in different parts of the world can make intercompany comparisons a highly hazardous undertaking.

Consider, for example, what happened in 1993 when the German company then known as Daimler-Benz took steps to list its common shares for trading on the New York Stock Exchange. Securities & Exchange Commission regulations dictate that any foreign company seeking a listing on a U.S. exchange must conform its accounting to the accounting regime most widely followed in the United States, known as U.S. GAAP (short for Generally Accepted Accounting Principles). When Daimler recast its financial statements to conform to GAAP, the company's reputation as one of the most consistently profitable global auto companies was suddenly imperiled. Under German rules the company had shown a profit in 1993 of 602 million Deutsche marks. But when results were computed using U.S. accounting methods, that profit was transformed into a loss of 1.8 billion marks, largely because of differences in U.S. and German methods of accounting for reserves. Similarly, British Airways' 1999 profit totaled $333 million using UK accounting procedures. Calculated under U.S. GAAP, profits came to only $168 million.

Simply bringing the results of foreign companies into conformity with U.S. principles does not assure that intercompany comparisons will be accurate or meaningful. Anyone comparing British Airways to Delta Airlines, a leading U.S. carrier, would likely conclude that Delta vastly outperformed BA in 1999, earning $7.20 per share, up 13 percent from the previous year, and posting a 24 percent return on equity. British Airways' results for the same period were earnings per share of 16.2 pence, down from 35.4 pence the year earlier, for a return on equity of 3.3 percent. But are the results really comparable? In 1999 Delta management decided to extend the useful life of its airplanes from 20 to 25 years, which cut the airline's depreciation charges by spreading the acquisition cost of its aircraft over a longer time span. The accounting decision — Delta's *second* revision of its fleet's useful life since 1988 — boosted EPS by $0.60. (Note the telltale sign of earnings management: $0.60 is a relatively small portion of overall earnings, but a major contributor to earnings *growth*. Without the change in useful life, EPS would have grown by only 4 percent.) Delta's numbers appear even less solid when you take into account the shorter average fleet life used by BA management when calculating depreciation charges. The point is, even numbers that appear directly comparable can be strongly influenced by assumptions that are not always apparent. Thus, before basing conclusions on benchmarks, make sure you know what went into the numbers.

In future years, direct comparison of U.S. and non-U.S. companies is likely to grow even more difficult. That difficulty is the perverse result of the efforts of both U.S. and international accounting authorities to improve reporting practices in the wake of the rolling series of financial-reporting scandals that began in 2001 and engulfed both U.S. and overseas corporations. The accounting treatment of intangible assets is likely to prove one of most stubborn impediments to direct comparison.

To gain a sense of the difficulty, consider the varying accounting treatments of the intangible asset known as goodwill. When one company acquires another, the acquirer usually pays a price higher than the market value of the acquired company's identifiable assets, such as inventories and equipment, net of any debt taken on. That premium over the net market value of identifiable assets is called *goodwill* and is reflected on the acquirer's books as an asset. In essence, goodwill captures any "unidentifiable assets" bought by the acquirer, as reflected in the price it paid for the other company. For example, if a company with $1 million of identifiable assets, net of debt, is acquired for $1.25 million, then goodwill of $250,000 is posted as an intangible asset on the acquirer's balance sheet. Theoretically, that $250,000 is the value of the acquired company's name and reputation, as well as any other intangible assets that cannot be identified and valued separately.

Under International Accounting Standards (IAS), the accounting regime followed by many European and Asian companies, corporations are required to amortize goodwill over a maximum of 20 years. Until recently, U.S. accounting principles also required that goodwill be written down gradually, although the maximum amortization period under U.S. GAAP was 40 years. The differing amortization periods notwithstanding, both IAS and U.S. GAAP viewed goodwill in essentially similar terms, as an asset that had a limited useful life. The two regimes disagreed only on the arbitrary point of where to set the limit.

New rules, however, have radically altered the treatment of goodwill under U.S. GAAP. Companies following U.S. GAAP must subject recognized goodwill to an annual impairment test. If the value of those assets has declined or been impaired for any reason, companies must write down the asset value immediately and record the write-down as an operating expense. Goodwill is no longer amortized. The new requirement has produced staggering write-downs: JDS Uniphase, one of the most acquisitive of the new economy networking companies, wrote down $40 billion of goodwill in 2001. In 2002, AOL Time Warner wrote down $53 billion of goodwill and warned that further write-downs were ahead. And in March 2003, WorldCom, formerly the highest of the telecom high-fliers, wrote off *all* the goodwill on its books—$45 billion—and took an additional $35 billion in write-offs on property, plant and equipment, and various other assets.

Although the International Accounting Standards Board is considering similar rules, as of this writing the practice of amortizing goodwill continues. Until goodwill accounting under IAS and U.S. GAAP converges, the differing treatments of intangibles will continue to make cross-border comparisons a hazardous undertaking. For example, the U.S. approach is likely to result in more volatile corporate earnings. But while some observers object to the volatility of earnings computed under U.S. guidelines, many investors and analysts may take such volatility as a sign that financial reporting has grown more reflective of a volatile reality, and thus more reliable.

Given the almost infinite number of variables that feed into any company's financial calculations, it is easy to see how an unwary investor or analyst could be misled about the relative performance of different companies. And indeed, managers are limited only by their imagination when it comes to devising new methods of misdirection. Like other accounting games, however, benchmark-related games tend to congregate into readily identifiable clusters. This chapter, therefore, will not attempt an exhaustive inventory of benchmarking sins and peccadilloes. We will point out where mischief is likely to occur and suggest how to spot the telltale signs of dubious benchmarking. We will also evaluate the various attempts now under way to make international methods of comparison more . . . well . . . comparable.

Benchmarking: The Tools of the Trade

The first thing to note about benchmarks is that there is no universally recognized benchmarking standard or set of guidelines. Over years of practice, however, the business community has developed an inventory of benchmarking tools that are in wide use. These tools allow comparisons between companies whose results could not otherwise be measured on the same scale. Some of the most widely used of those tools are listed and defined below. (This list, by the way, is not exhaustive. Many benchmarks are industry-specific. For example, airlines frequently gauge their performance by revenue per passenger seat-mile, which is a way of measuring the average amount of revenue generated by each paying customer. This metric, or ones like it, would be of no use or relevance in most other industries.)

The first and most important measure is **return on equity** (**ROE**) sometimes referred to as return on common shareholders' equity. ROE is defined as the ratio of net income to shareholders' equity, which is in turn defined as total assets less total liabilities.

A popular alternative to ROE is **return on invested capital**, which is defined as operating income (pretax or aftertax deepening on the preference of the analyst) divided by invested capital. Invested capital is normally defined as the sum of shareholders' equity and debt—or, if one prefers an asset-based perspective, the sum of long-term assets, working capital (such as inventories and receivables), and cash. The main difference between ROE and ROIC is that the former focuses on returns to shareholders, while the latter considers all capital providers. In other words, ROIC measures returns on all contributed capital independently of whether the capital is in the form of equity or debt. What the two measures have in common is that they are the most direct methods of determining what investors are getting in return for their money.

Another widely used measure is **asset turnover**, which is sales as a percentage of assets. It is an indicator of the efficiency with which management deploys the enterprise's assets. The fewer the assets employed per dollar of sales, the greater the asset turnover and the greater the ROIC and ROE.

Net profit margin is simply the ratio of net income to sales. Gross margin, another popular measure, is gross profit (usually defined as sales minus cost of sales) divided by sales. Operating margin is the ratio of operating income to sales. Among other things, margins measure how effectively a company can control its costs.

Several financial ratios measure the level of indebtedness incurred by a given company. Common ratios include **debt as a percentage of equity** and **debt as a percentage of assets**. Comparison of such ratios among different companies can help observers assess the risk level of a given firm and the extent of its remaining borrowing capacity. **Coverage tests** include the ratio of operating income **to interest due** (or interest and principal), as well as the ratio of **cash before interest and taxes to interest due** (or interest and principal). Such measures help investors and lenders determine whether a company is generating sufficient income to cover interest expense and principal payments.

Income-statement relationships are another widely used set of metrics. In addition to net profit, gross, and operating profit margins, cost efficiency can be measured by the ratio of selling, general and administrative expenses **(SG&A) to sales.** A company's commitment to innovation can be roughly measured by comparing **research and development expenses to sales.**

Finally, some benchmarks track trends by comparing balance-sheet or income-statement information from one period to the same information from another period. In particular, year-to-year sales growth is a key indicator that drives sales estimates, earnings forecasts, and, in many cases, executive compensation.

How Benchmarks Can Mislead

Managers who wish to tweak these widely used benchmarks to yield misleading information have a nearly infinite range of options available to them. Consider the metric known as return on equity. One component of the ROE calculation is, of course, earnings. In earlier chapters we examined in some detail how managerial decisions about everything from revenue recognition to provisions for future costs to estimated pension-fund returns can ratchet earnings up or down. Every managerial decision that results in a less-than-reliable earnings number will also produce a less-than-reliable ROE number.

That said, however, it is worth looking at a few of the methods companies have historically used to prettify their benchmarks. As we noted earlier, Delta Airlines in 1999 increased the useful life of its airplanes to 25 years from 20—and this move followed Delta management's 1988 decision to increase the useful life of its planes from 15 years to 20. The 1999 decision allowed Delta to report a return on equity of 24 percent—ROE would have been 22 percent without the change in Delta's useful-life assumption. Germany's Lufthansa in the same period reported a return on equity identical to Delta's, leading the unwary observer to conclude that both air carriers were equally adept stewards of shareholder equity. Yet Lufthansa's useful life estimates were only 12 years, less than half the useful life assumed by Delta. Without knowing the accounting decisions underlying the earnings number that feeds into ROE calculation, an investor or analyst could easily conclude that Delta's performance was roughly equal to Lufthansa's. A closer look into the makeup of those ROE numbers, however, would lead to the conclusion that Lufthansa was generating a higher return on shareholders' equity.

In attempting to improve their return on assets, most companies focus on the numerator in the equation—the earnings figure that, when divided by assets, determines the return. But Enron, innovative as ever, focused on reducing the denominator, which would have the same effect as increasing the numerator—an improvement in ROA. Reducing the denominator was, in fact, the essence of Enron's "asset-lite" strategy. Like most things Enron, the strategy was a sham. The numbers that Enron fed into its ROA calculations were suspect or downright fraudulent. Even after being fudged, Enron's benchmark ratios were unimpressive: At the peak of its period of megagrowth, which lasted from 1999 until mid-2001, Enron's ROIC was a paltry 7 percent or so, and its operating profit margin was only 2 percent. In other words, despite their Harvard MBAs, despite their experience at such high-powered firms as McKinsey & Co. and Arthur Andersen, and despite their insistence on referring to their organization as "the world's leading company," Enron's managers were just not very good at running a profitable business.

As a result of its off-balance-sheet entities and other methods, Enron also effectively falsified its interest-coverage calculations. Anyone attempting to evaluate the company's creditworthiness would have been hard-pressed to judge the company's ability to repay its debts, given that it hid so many borrowings in off-balance-sheet entities and disguised other loans as asset sales. But had the credit-rating agencies made a closer study of Enron's statement of cash flows, they might have sounded the alarm sooner. They would have seen Enron's cash and its earnings headed in opposite directions—or, like *Fortune* magazine reporter Bethany McClean, they might simply have confessed that they couldn't figure out how the company made its money. It appears that the credit-rating agencies, whose fees are paid by the companies they examine, were as intimidated by Enron management as were the analysts who took Enron's numbers on faith rather than admit they didn't "get it."

Common Sense: The Ultimate Benchmark

The collapse of Enron, and the revelation that the company was little more than a sham resting on a fraud and wrapped in a fiction, points up vividly that the one indispensable benchmark is common sense and skepticism. You didn't have to be a financial Sherlock Holmes to ask how Enron's revenue could have grown from $39 billion in 1999 to $100 billion in 2000—a one-year improvement of 155 percent. Such rates of growth are not unprecedented, of course—but companies that grow at such a rapid rate are almost invariably startups, not mature companies.

The same sorts of questions should have been asked by those responsible for reporting the financial results of Lernout & Hauspie, the Belgian developer of voice-recognition software. The company's sales in South Korea jumped from $97,000 in the first quarter of 1999 to $59 million in the first quarter of 2000—a one-year increase of 60,000 percent. Common sense alone should have prompted experienced observers to wonder how a subsidiary's revenue could explode so dramatically. Where were the skeptics to warn that the purported growth occurred in South Korea, a country with a history of aggressive accounting and financial scandal? And why was a Lehman Brothers software analyst the only one to ask if the South Korean market for voice-recognition software was large and robust enough to generate $59 million of demand for a single company? By September 2000, when it became clear that Lernout & Hauspie's financial reports were full of holes, the company's share price had fallen to $15, from a high of $73 in March 2000. Liquidation followed soon thereafter.

Corporate insiders and outside observers alike need a thorough grounding in the benchmarks used by a particular organization, not only to understand the terms by which one company compares itself to others, but also because companies use benchmarks to manage themselves and reward their employees. These benchmarks are supposed to give employees incentives to advance the corporation's aims. In all too many cases, however, benchmarks distort corporate strategy and bring about results that are diametrically opposed to stated corporate goals.

Once again, Enron provides a handy example of the perverse outcomes that badly designed, poorly thought-out benchmarks can produce. The pay of executives of Enron's energy services division, which managed energy for large companies like Eli Lilly, was figured on the basis of long-term value of energy services contracts. But estimates of contract value were internally generated. Thus, energy services executives had a compelling incentive to pump up the purported value of the contracts, whether or not the cash promised by such estimates ever materialized.

Enron isn't the only company to be led astray by the wrong set of pay benchmarks. In March 2003, BristolMyers Squibb (BMS), a U.S. pharmaceuticals company, announced a $2.5 billion downward revision of sales from 1999 through 2001, and a $900 million downward revision of earnings over the same period. Behind the restatement lay a classic channel-stuffing scheme: BMS executives would offer incentives to wholesalers to take additional inventory, which would allow the executives to claim they had met their quarterly sales targets. The drugs were, in effect, delivered to wholesalers on consignment—meaning that BMS should not have recognized revenue on the drugs until the wholesalers had resold them and remitted payment to BMS. When BMS instead recognized revenue at the time of shipment, it committed the quintessential accounting no-no.

Here's what makes this story more than just another account of garden-variety channel stuffing: In 1999, BMS changed its managerial compensation scheme to one that rewarded sales growth rather than total return to shareholders (capital appreciation plus dividend yield). By changing its benchmarks, BMS essentially invited its managers to pump up their sales numbers by any means necessary.

The BMS case is just one example of the pernicious effect that ill-chosen benchmarks can have on executive pay. Compensation consultants routinely use the pay of other CEOs as a key benchmark. Well aware of this fact, senior executives cheer every time one of their peers gets a fat raise. Are they celebrating a colleague's good fortune? Hardly—that's rather more altruism than you can expect from a senior corporate manager. Rather, each upward bump in executive pay nudges the standard of comparison a little higher, allowing even poorly performing executives to demand higher pay—after all, their compensation packages must remain "competitive."

Perhaps the most blatant recent illustration of the way the rising tide of executive pay lifts all senior managerial boats is the 2002 pay package awarded to Delta CEO Leo Mullin. Although Delta lost $1.27 billion in 2002, Mullin was awarded cash, stock, and other compensation worth some $13 million, more than twice his take in 2001. Delta's justification for its largesse: Other airlines did even worse than Delta in 2002. Besides, other senior airline executives won big raises, and Mullin's package had to keep pace. We hear a great deal about the stress executives suffer. It must come as great consolation to these executives that, thanks to creative benchmarking, they need not perform well to "earn" a big raise—they only need perform less badly than their peers.

Benchmarking and Corporate Governance

What links Mullin's raise, Enron's fraud, and the restatement fiasco at BristolMyers Squibb is that, in each case, the board of directors could have blocked management and did not. Where was Enron's board when the company allowed pay to be determined by internally generated estimates? Where was the board of directors when BMS management proposed changing its compensation benchmarks? And where were the voices of reason on Delta's compensation committee, the board subgroup that by U.S. statute is responsible for determining senior executive compensation and for overseeing the corporation's overall pay standards and practices? Did any BMS directors point out the risks and potential unintended consequences of the company's decision to change its managerial incentives? Did they examine the historical record to learn from the experience of other companies that had effected similar changes in their incentive programs? Did the members of Delta's compensation committee fulfill their fiduciary duty to shareholders?

The problem is, shareholders are rarely present in large numbers when directors get together. When directors meet, they usually do so under the gaze of the CEO—the person who recruited them, determines their compensation, and controls most of the corporate information that reaches them. The CEO may have business or social ties to directors, although new stock-exchange regulations and the Sarbanes-Oxley Act of 2002 set some limits on those ties. Even without such ties, the pressure to defer to the CEO, as leader of the corporation, can be intense. Indeed, in the dynamics of group psychology we find a likely explanation for the extraordinary passivity, incuriosity, and malleability of boards like those of Enron, Delta, and Bristol-Myers Squibb.

Psychologists have long known of the power of peer pressure. In one famous experiment, conducted by pioneering psychologist Solomon Asch, test subjects were shown drawings of parallel lines. The subjects were asked to measure the lines to determine for themselves that the lines were of equal length. Asch then embellished one line with an inward-facing arrow at each end and the other line with an outward-facing arrow at each end. He thus created a well-known optical illusion: The line with the outward-facing arrows appears longer. Two collaborators of Asch then joined the test subject and insisted that the line with the outward-facing arrows was longer than the other line. By repeatedly asserting the unequal length of the lines and questioning the intelligence of anyone who would argue otherwise, the experimenters wore down the subject until he or she agreed that one line was indeed longer than the other—*even though the subject had measured the lines and knew them to be of equal length.*

Now extend Asch's unnerving insight about the power of peer pressure into the Enron boardroom. Enron CEO Jeffrey Skilling rarely disguised his haughty scorn for those who "didn't get it"—didn't swallow the company's jargon-ridden nonexplanations for how it made its money. Chairman Kenneth Lay's preferred method of persuasion, by contrast, was affability and a bottomless faith in the near-mystical wisdom of free markets. In the face of a good-cop, bad-cop act like that of Lay and Skilling, how many people would have the emotional fortitude to stand up before their peers and ask uncomfortable questions about Enron's numbers? That is why the new laws and regulations requiring independence and financial literacy of corporate directors may not be enough, though they will doubtless lead to improvements over earlier practices. Regulators and legislators may be able to establish financial thresholds for independence and strict definitions of financial literacy, but they cannot measure or mandate the skepticism, persistence, and emotional security needed to stand up to the ferocious pressure generated by a high-powered peer group such as a corporate board.

Of course, the vagaries of group psychology do not excuse board misfeasance, nor do they doom boards to supine incompetence. Boards can move proactively on the vital question of benchmarks by keeping one question at the front of their minds as they deliberate: **Are there differences between their company's financial reports and those of its competitors that must be disclosed to ensure that the shareholder's interests are fairly considered?**

Other questions flow from that one key interrogative. Board members must be prepared to press management and auditors for answers to the following:

Do the financial statements fairly compare the company's financial performance with prior results, budgets, and competitors?

Are there aspects of the company's accounting methods that might skew performance benchmarks and give an inaccurate impression of the company's financial performance?

Do the financial statements address possible distortions induced by accounting methods?

Are accounting methods consistent from year to year? Are they consistent with general industry practice? Where accounting methods differ from competitors', what is the supporting rationale for the deviation? Are the differences adequately disclosed and discussed?

Who is responsible for establishing the benchmarks by which a corporation assesses its performance? Directors have an obligation to shareholders to ask whether a corporate officer who stands to gain from the attainment of particular benchmarks should choose and calculate those benchmarks. The directors who make up the compensation committee are also responsible for ensuring that the benefits consultants engaged by the committee are benchmarking appropriately. In comparing the corporation's performance against that of its competitors, have the consultants factored in variances in competitors' accounting judgments?

These are the questions that an effective board would raise. The experience of the past several years, however, has demonstrated that investors, analysts, journalists, and other outside parties cannot assume that boards will do the job they are paid to do. Outsiders who wish to do their own review of a company's benchmarking practices can use the following list of questions.

Which competitors should the company be measured against? Most companies describe their competition in their financial reports such as 10-K filings and proxy statements. But don't stop there. Management's categories of comparison are often narrowly tailored to make their company come out on top. For example, management of a publicly held sports team may want to limit the comparison to other sports teams. But a more accurate comparison may be to other providers of leisure-time entertainment, such as movie theaters, theme restaurants, and amusement parks.

Do the firms under comparison all adhere to the same accounting regime, such as IAS or U.S. GAAP? If differing regimes are being employed, the accounting will have to be adjusted to eliminate the distortions introduced by differing treatment of items such as goodwill.

Are the reports of competitors reliable, or do the reporting and auditing practices in their business environment raise doubts about the reliability of their financial statements? Some countries, such as Japan, are notoriously lax about requiring accurate disclosure of bad debts. Others, such as South Korea, leave much to be desired in their disclosure of related-party transactions. Moreover, many disclosures that U.S. investors take for granted are unheard-of in other countries. Until recently, for example, Swiss companies were not required to make any disclosures regarding executive compensation. And the accounting systems in place in most countries do not call for management's discussion and analysis (MD&A) of financial results. The MD&A is often the most valuable section of U.S. annual reports. Interestingly, although U.S. companies are indeed required to include an MD&A in their annual reports, U.S. GAAP does not demand that they do so. Rather, it is mandated by the Securities & Exchange Commission.

Does the company under examination clearly disclose significant differences between its financial reports and those of competitors? If a U.S. company's main rivals are in Europe, for instance, does the U.S. company acknowledge the differences in reporting systems between European and U.S. accounting systems? Does it provide an estimate of the impact of those differences on its financial statements? (In this regard, Microsoft offers a useful model for other companies to follow. It presents its earnings and balance-sheet data as figured using seven different accounting systems—U.S. GAAP and six others—and a range of accounting choices. It also translates its results into different currencies.)

Corporations should also make an effort to ensure that rankings and lists such as the Fortune 500 and Global 1000 do not over- or understate corporate performance. Bear in mind that the greater the number of companies under comparison, the more plentiful the opportunities for distortion.

9

LET'S MAKE UP SOME NUMBERS: EBITDA, PRO FORMA EARNINGS, AND STUPID CASH TRICKS

$\mathbf{M}$ost of this book is taken up in discussion of the various techniques that accountants and corporate managers can (and do) employ to paint a misleading picture of a company's financial condition. Management can overstate revenue or understate expenses, pass off one-time windfalls as recurring gains or, conversely, disguise recurring losses as singular events. But sometimes even those methods aren't sufficient to produce the desired results: profits, or at least the appearance of profits. Does management then simply give up and admit the sad financial truth? Not likely. More often, something other than profitability—something usually called EBITDA or pro forma earnings—becomes the appropriate measure of the firm's well-being.

Welcome to accounting's looking-glass world, where losses are magically transformed into gains and inconvenient financial facts that can't be explained away are simply ignored. Even cash flow, which conventional wisdom says can't be faked, turns out to be vulnerable to distortion and gimmickry. In this chapter, we will examine the good (cash flow), the bad (pro forma), and the ugly (EBITDA), and the way corporate managers use or abuse these financial measures to deceive lenders, investors, and, ultimately, themselves. We will review the arguments in favor of EBITDA and other alternative performance measures and explain why we find them unconvincing. But first, a little history.

Like other accounting games, alternative-measurement games started long before the hyperboom of the late 1990s. EBITDA—which stands for Earnings Before Interest, Taxes, Depreciation, and Amortization—came into wide use among private capital firms when calculating what to pay for a business. Such firms referred to price-to-EBITDA ratios as frequently as a stock-market investor would refer to price-to-earnings ratios. But EBITDA didn't gain currency among public companies until the merger wave of the 1980s, when companies such as Time Warner encouraged analysts and journalists to use the measure to evaluate corporate performance. EBITDA, the argument went, stripped out the noncash costs associated with acquisitions, leaving only the cash return generated by a firm's ongoing operations.

Many analysts and reporters bought that reasoning, and so did many executives. At one takeover-happy corporation after another, senior management latched onto EBITDA as a way to cushion the impact of corporate spending sprees. At the time, few journalists or analysts had the impertinence to point out that mergers and acquisitions were, in fact, a major line of business at many companies, and that takeover-related costs themselves should logically be incorporated into results from continuing operations. Lacking a serious challenger in the marketplace of ideas, EBITDA became a widely accepted measure. It was especially popular during the late 1990s, the golden age of financial gimmickry. The technology companies that were the stock market's darlings enthusiastically embraced EBITDA, claiming it as yet another example of the advanced mindset that guaranteed their triumph over the dinosaurs of the old economy.

The chief financial officer of Cadence Systems was refreshingly honest about his company's decision to discuss only EBITDA in its press releases, eliminating all reference to net income as calculated using conventional accounting. Cadence CFO Bill Porter asserted that the conventional numbers would appear in the company's SEC filings, and that citing two different earnings numbers in a press release would only confuse investors. "Long, wordy press releases are not things that people look at," he told the *Wall Street Journal*. "Investors say, 'keep it short and simple.'" He has a point: Investors do tend to seek a single bottom line. And if a business can choose its own bottom line, is it more likely to choose the more accurate number, or the more flattering one?

Pro forma earnings have a much older lineage than EBITDA, and, it might be argued, a more honorable one. For decades, companies have reported pro forma earnings in the first year or so following a merger, adjusting results from earlier periods to show what revenue and profits would have looked like if the combination had already been in place. The exercise was more than academic—it permitted investors to compare current results against results from earlier periods. For example, a corporation with $1 billion in revenue that had just acquired a rival with $600 million in sales would report pro forma numbers so that the public could meaningfully compare the combined companies' $1.6 billion in sales with results from earlier periods.

The problem is, the term "pro forma" means different things to different people. Some companies use "pro forma" to refer to operating earnings, which is to say earnings derived from ordinary business activities. Such companies compare those "pro forma" earnings with net income, which includes operating earnings as well as gains and losses that fall outside the range of ordinary business. In yet another context, "pro forma" refers to the projected earnings, cash flows, and balance sheets that investors and lenders use to evaluate the potential of the business. When bankers or venture capitalists ask to see the pro formas, they are referring to those projections.

Our comments apply only to "pro forma" as the term was used— and abused—during and after the dot-com era. In the 1990s, the dot-coms and other highly speculative enterprises found the pro forma designation useful precisely because of its vagueness and imprecision. Internet entrepreneurs, investment bankers, and their tame analysts all had strong incentives to make financially unsound businesses appear valuable, or at least potentially so, and pro forma earnings were a handy means to that end. They were also a handy way to discourage unwelcome scrutiny. Rather than use pro forma accounting to enable investors to compare results from different time periods, many technology companies used it to frustrate comparison, often obscuring or omitting the ways in which their pro forma results diverged from results obtained using standard accounting methods.

It may seem strange, in retrospect, that so many corporations during the boom resorted to such a transparent device to divert attention

away from their true financial condition, and even stranger that so many
analysts, investors, and business journalists fell for it. But during buying
panics like that of the late 1990s, dubious judgment becomes conta-
gious. At the time, many business gurus were urging old-line companies
to adopt the dot-com mindset. Many companies took heed, adopting the
mindset as well as the dot-coms' style of financial reporting, both of
which came with a large dose of wishful thinking.

And we do mean large. One study found that among 100 high
technology companies traded on Nasdaq and filing financial reports in
the first three quarters of 2001, there was a cumulative $100 billion dif-
ference between pro forma profits and profits as calculated using standard accounting. Through the magic of pro forma, $20 billion of losses,
as figured under GAAP, were transformed into profits of $80 billion.
Meanwhile, between 1999 and 2001, the number of companies reporting on a pro forma basis tripled, to 1,500. *Forbes* magazine compiled a
list of some of the most egregious pro forma results of 2001, highlight-
ing the difference between pro forma and more orthodox profits. Not
surprisingly, a telecommunications company led the list: Level 3 Communications reported a pro forma loss of $1.24 per share, which, as loss-
es go, is far preferable to $16.20-per-share loss it posted using grown-
up accounting.

Humbled high-fliers from the tech sector weren't the only ones
with big gaps between their conventional numbers and the numbers they
wanted markets and the media to focus on. More established companies
played the pro forma game, too. The magic of pro forma transformed Fed-
erated Department Stores' $1.33-per-share loss to a profit of $3.03, and
CMS Energy's $4.17-per-share loss looked much better as a pro forma
$1.41 profit. As these instances might suggest, the first rule of pro forma
earnings is: The bigger the difference between pro forma and GAAP earnings, the more you should worry about the reliability of either number.

Pro forma earnings are especially valuable for concocting price-
to-earnings ratios that appear almost reasonable to unwary investors.
Standard & Poor's Corp. has calculated that in 2001, the shares of companies reporting pro forma earnings had an average price-to-earnings ratio of 24, not far from the p/e ratio of blue-chip companies. But that's
only when calculating the ratio based on pro forma numbers. Calculating
the ratio using conventional U.S. accounting methods yields a price-earn-
ings ratio of 37—far more typical of a speculative company with a volatile stock price.

Still, pro forma reporting—or as Lynn Turner, former chief accountant of the SEC, put it, "earnings without the bad stuff"—might have some limited usefulness if it were clear what bad stuff was being left out. New regulations require that companies disclose what are called "reconciling items," the charges and gains that have for various reasons been excluded from the pro forma calculation. The change was prompted by abuses like the one perpetrated by Trump Hotels, which in 1999 reported pro forma earnings that beat Wall Street expectations, thanks in large part to a $17 million, one-time gain from the sale of equipment. The pro forma report didn't mention an offsetting $81 million charge for discontinued operations. When the SEC discovered this omission, it censured—but did not fine—Trump Hotels and required the company to issue a clarifying press release. Earnings without the bad stuff, indeed.

The SEC requirement that companies report their reconciling items is a sign of progress, but it doesn't go far enough. For example, there's no requirement to include reconciling items from earlier periods. Without such items, it's impossible to make useful year-to-year earnings comparisons or comparisons with competitors. In our view, the best thing to do with pro forma numbers is to ridicule or ignore them, unless they're the old-fashioned kind—financial reports designed to enable comparison rather than thwart it.

In 2002 Standard & Poor's Corp. introduced a new alternative performance measure, which it calls core earnings. In its calculation, S&P includes some restructuring expenses, if they are incurred in the ordinary course of business, as well as hedging expenses and merger expenses, which companies usually do not classify as operating expenses, even when they are basic to the business. S&P also expenses employee stock options and adjusts pension expense to a more realistic level. Designed to correct for management's inherently self-serving bias, core earnings tend to fall far below the earnings companies actually report. In October 2002, says S&P, the stock market was priced at 54 times core earnings, compared with 37 percent reported earnings and 24 percent pro forma earnings. By that measure, the stock market still had room to fall, and fall it did.

The core earnings measure is a good-faith, knowledgeable attempt at a fair measure of relative performance, but it is hardly flawless. Like pro forma numbers, core earnings cannot be easily compared from one year to the next, and comparisons between companies can also be skewed. But it is still a useful way to "reality-test" the numbers that corporate management reports. Had Enron's core earnings been calculated, its option and pension expenses would have transformed profits to losses, and investors and regulators might have been able to act while there were still significant assets to preserve.

The Twisting of EBITDA

As we said earlier, EBITDA was originally employed by private capital firms as a valuation tool. The firms had three reasons for removing interest, taxes, depreciation, and amortization from their earnings calculations. They removed taxes because they wanted to substitute their own tax-rate calculations. Amortization was excluded because it measured the cost of intangible assets acquired in some earlier period rather than any current expenditure of cash. Depreciation, an indirect and backward-looking measure of capital expenditure, was excluded and replaced with an estimate of future capital expenditure. In sum, private capital firms stripped out interest, taxes, and depreciation because they were going to replace them with their own, presumably more precise numbers.

EBITDA applied to public companies is a very different matter. First of all, rather than use the number to value entire companies, as private capitalists do, public companies and analysts encourage investors to use EBITDA to value shares of stock. Unlike private capitalists, though, most stock investors don't substitute their own numbers for the numbers that EBITDA drops. Instead, they simply exclude from earnings calculations a mixed bag of cash and noncash charges to arrive at an earnings measure that fails to reflect the realities of running a public business. Compounding this problem, many analysts and journalists urge investors to use EBITDA as a measure of the cash a business generates. Such a contention is illogical, misleading, and hazardous to investors' wealth.

Here's why EBITDA is a flawed estimate of cash flows and an incoherent measure of earnings. First, let's concede that if the goal is to estimate how much cash is generated by operations, it is necessary (though not sufficient) to remove noncash expenses—i.e., depreciation and amortization—from the income statement. Depreciation and amortization appear on the income statement as expenses that reflect the use of fixed assets, such as machinery and real estate, and intangible assets such as patents and brand equity. Cash was paid for those assets in the past, and the payment was reflected as a use of cash in the investment section of the cash-flow statement. Every year, the value of those assets is written down (or amortized or depreciated) by a fixed percentage. The amount of the decrease is then deducted, like other expenses, from earnings. But the decrease in earnings doesn't alter the corporation's cash position. Clearly, then, such noncash expenses need to be added back to net earnings to arrive at an estimate of cash flow from operations.

If EBITDA stopped there, it might have some limited use — severely limited, for reasons we will explain. But EBITDA doesn't stop there. It excludes taxes, which are a real cash item, and not at all optional — a company that doesn't write its tax check to the government won't stay in business long. True, for various reasons the amount of the check often differs from the expense recorded on the income statement, but the appropriate adjustment is not to simply ignore the reported tax expense. Instead, a careful investor or analyst would replace the tax expense on the income statement with the cash outlay found in the "taxes paid" line of the operating cash-flow statement. That operation would yield a far more accurate estimate of the cash available for capital expenditures and dividends. But the estimate would still be flawed, because EBITDA does not exclude all noncash items, only depreciation and amortization. Among the noncash items not adjusted for in EBITDA are warranty expenses, bad debt allowances, inventory write-downs, and the cost of stock options granted. That last item may soon prove to be a significant omission.

The question of whether stock options should be accounted for as an expense has recently been the subject of considerable controversy. Those opposed to expensing options (including many technology-company executives) argue that it is difficult to measure the true value of stock options, especially when the issuer is a young enterprise with uncertain prospects. But even if figuring the value of the option is an inexact science, both issuer and employee believe the options have value, as the case of German company SAP demonstrates. The software firm does not issue stock options to executives in its home country, where the tax code discourages that form of compensation. When SAP first expanded to the United States, it attempted to recruit a cadre of American executives without offering stock options. Shortly after losing several of its top officers to rivals offering options packages, SAP brought its U.S. policies into line with local compensation practices. If those departed

SAP managers believed options had no value, they wouldn't have left their SAP posts for jobs that offered options.

If we accept the obvious—that options have value—it would seem to follow that corporations should account for options grants as an expense. That is, after all, what corporations usually do when they part with money or something else of value. But to date, U.S. accounting rules have not required corporations to take that logical step. Instead, the rules give companies the choice of expensing stock options or disclosing in a footnote the impact they would have on earnings. Until recently, nearly every company took the footnote route, with such notable exceptions as Boeing and Winn-Dixie, which have included options as an expense on their income statements, reducing earnings per share. No company wanted to be the first to start expensing options, figuring that the move would put it at a competitive disadvantage. But in the wake of serial corporate scandals, leading corporations such as Coca-Cola, and General Electric have started to expense their options. Their actions have emboldened many other companies to follow suit. Investors have ratcheted up pressure on the laggards, penalizing the shares of companies that don't account for their options that way. In this fashion, market forces have begun to bring about a de facto change in accounting conventions. When U.S. and international standard-setting bodies eventually do promulgate new rules regarding options expenses, they may do little more than ratify a widely accepted process.

Of course, companies have for years repored their stock option expenses in the footnotes to their financial statements, so it is by no means certain that new reporting requirements will change corporate behavior. It seems reasonable to expect a search for the otions-valuation method that will minimize expense and maximize income. In addition, the compensation committees of some corporations may begin to explicitly consider options expenses in their executive-awards calculations, but there is little evidence to that effect as this book goes to press.

What do options expenses have to do with EBITDA? This: They are a noncash expense that will appear in numerous financial statements and may be a significant expense in many young, technology-based businesses. If EBITDA is to have any utility as an estimate of cash from operations, it will have to take account of stock options. In this case, we may soon have a new abbreviation to remember—EBITDAS, where the S stands for stock-based compensation.

As if this weren't enough, EBITDA is plagued by another flaw. Unlike proper measures of cash flow, it ignores changes in working capital. This lacuna is especially troubling in cases of fast-growing companies. Such enterprises require increased investment in receivables and inventories to convert their growth potential into sales. These investments consume cash, just like any other. Even if we were to make EBITDA an after-tax measure, and adjust for other potential distortions, its failure to consider changes in working capital makes it a poor substitute for operating cash flows.

Of all EBITDA's flaws, however, the most grievous is its vulnerability to the same accounting games found on the income statement (except for games related to depreciation and taxes). In other words, even if you correct for distortions in T, D, and A, the E in EBITDA may be unreliable. If a company has over- or underreserved for warranty costs, restructuring expenses, or bad-debt allowances, its earnings will be skewed and its EBITDA misleading. If it has recognized revenue prematurely or disguised ordinary costs as capital investments, its numbers will be suspect. If it has inflated revenue through round-trip asset trades, the E will be of little informational value.

Indeed, the informational value of EBITDA itself seems questionable. As an estimate of cash flow it suffers from conceptual flaws we believe to be fatal: It excludes cash tax payments; it includes possibly substantial noncash expenses; and it requires unquestioning acceptance of earnings numbers that deserve to be met with the severest skepticism. Besides, it's unnecessary. If you want to know the cash flow from operations, you should (carefully and skeptically) examine the cash-flow statement. That's what it's there for.

The Class System of Cash: Where the Games Are

The standard line on Wall Street is that you can fake revenue and profits, but you can't fake cash. And that's true—sort of. Assuming that reasonable financial controls are in place and that the internal and external audit staffs are honest (alas, no longer an unquestioned assumption), all the cash on the cash-flow statement is real. But that doesn't mean that the cash-flow statement is immune from fakery and deception.

Under the accounting regimes most widely followed in Europe and the United States cash flow falls into three categories—operations, investment, and financing. There are a few slight differences in classification, but these differences are plain and easy to adjust for. The most important category, when valuing a business, is cash flow from operations. That's the number investors and lenders look at to assess a company's ability to cover capital expenditures and pay dividends to shareholders. It can be in a company's interest to make that number look as large as possible. As we shall see, there are several ways to accomplish that task, using either nonrecurring items or cash that shouldn't really be considered cash from operations.

Consider how Microsoft, a corporation generally acknowledged as a model of responsible reporting, maximizes its reported operating cash flows. In 2001, according to the company's annual report, the software maker's operating cash flow was $11.4 billion.

Or was it?

One source of operating cash on the Microsoft statement is the tax benefit from the exercise of stock options. Here's how Microsoft captures that benefit: The company pays no tax and incurs no expense when it issues options to employees to buy stock at the current market price. Similarly, employees incur no tax liability upon exercising the option. But employees do pay capital gains tax when they profitably sell the shares they acquired through the exercise of options. That's not surprising. But you may be surprised to learn that accounting rules allow Microsoft to treat the amount of the employees' profit as an expense—just like a cash wage or salary—and reduce its taxable income accordingly. In 2001, when Microsoft shares were skyrocketing and many employees were cashing in, Microsoft enjoyed a $5.5 billion tax benefit – almost half its entire operating cash flow. This cash is indisputably cash from operations, but unlike other operating cash flows, it may not be sustainable. Indeed, it was not: In 2002, Microsoft's cash flow from employee options exercises fell about 50 percent from the previous year. Microsoft can continue to enjoy the tax break only as long as its stock price keeps rising and its employees continue to convert their options. This has important implications for anyone attempting to value the company based on projected future cash flows.

Another dubious entry on many operating cash-flow statements is the line on taxes paid. At some companies, a significant portion of tax liabilities is generated by transactions unrelated to operations. For example, the tax impact of gains or losses from the sale of assets is reflected in operating cash flow, even though the transaction itself is an investment activity. There may also be taxes related to corporate acqui-sitions or divestitures. Again, those activities involve a real cash bene-fit, but it is misleading to say that the benefit is comparable to tax savings from paying salaries, receiving payments from customers, and buying inventory.

The purchase and sale of securities can also distort the operating cash-flow statement. When a corporation purchases securities issued by another organization, it can designate them as either trading securi-ties or securities available for sale. *Trading securities*, as their name implies, are those bought or sold in short-term transactions designed to capture trading profits (or losses, in some cases). *Securities available for sale*, by contrast, are those that the corporation plans to hold for some time, possibly with longer-term strategic intent. For example, the French luxury-goods marketer LVMH purchased $1.4 billion of Gucci shares in 1999. The purchase was, in fact, LVMH's first shot in what turned out to be an attempt to take over Gucci. But when Gucci suc-ceeded in fending off LVMH, the French company dropped its bid and sold its shares at a profit. (The French company benefited from a bit of gruesome good timing, completing its sale on September 10, 2001.) Had LVMH designated the Gucci shares as trading securities, as man-agement had the discretion to do, the proceeds of the sale would have appeared as cash from operations.

LVMH categorized the Gucci shares as securities available for sale, and thus the proceeds from their sale appeared in the investment section of LVMH's cash-flow statement. But at some companies, man-agement plays games with trading securities, managing cash flow by pur-chasing securities to soak up excess cash during flush periods and selling when cash flow weakens. Without a closer look at the reported details in the cash-flow statement, a reader could conclude that a surge in cash rep-resents healthy growth rather than the proceeds of stock and bond trades.

Research and development expenses can also be manipulated to game cash flow. United States accounting regulations require compa-nies to book R&D costs as an expense until there is evidence that the R&D has resulted in a product ready for sale. At that point, research costs can be shifted to the balance sheet and capitalized—that is, treated as a capital investment. Of course, when the costs move to the balance sheet, they no longer reduce earnings. What's more, the shift of the ex-penditure to the investment section of the cash report has the effect of increasing operating cash flow. No wonder corporate managers are sometimes tempted to abuse their discretion to designate when a product is ready for sale. As we saw in Chapter 6, Kendall Square Research declared it had a product ready for sale just as it was issuing a final earnings report prior to its initial public offering. The shift of costs from expenses to capital investment helped Kendall Square report a profit, and its IPO was a success, if only briefly.

Tyco, the conglomerate whose former CEO, Dennis Kozlowski, has been accused of a variety of misdeeds including tax evasion, is another company that has juggled the cash categories to paint a misleading picture of its operations. Consider the way the company's ADT home-security unit handles its customer-acquisition costs. When it acquires customers through its own in-house sales, promotion, and marketing efforts, the costs of those efforts are deducted from operating cash. But when it acquired 800,000 new customers from third-party distributors, ADT classified the $830 million expenditure as an investment, which reduced the cash in the investment category but left operating cash untouched. What's more, when customers' fees for those systems began to flow in, ADT recorded them as operating cash. The treatment is defensible, but it overstates the company's cash flow in comparison to competitors that treat all their customer-acquisitions as reductions in operating cash.

Construction costs and costs related to self-constructed assets can also cloud the cash picture. In the ordinary course of business, interest expense and employee salary and fringes are treated as an expense that reduces net earnings. But during construction, interest costs move to the investments section, thus increasing operating cash flow and earnings. Likewise, the internal costs of personnel involved in constructing or installing plant are added to investments instead of being treated as an operating expense, with a concomitant increase in earnings and operating cash flow. Analysts and investors need to be wary, because once construction is complete, the costs will again be treated as expenses, with corresponding reductions in earnings and operating cash flow.

One popular strategy is to sell or securitize receivables. When the sale is correctly structured, the receivables disappear from the balance sheet, replaced by cash. This approach is a well-recognized example of off-balance-sheet financing. Although the accounting treatment and precise legal details may differ, securitizing receivables is little different from short-term borrowing collateralized by receivables. But rather than being classified as financing cash flow, the loan is categorized as operating cash flow. Any time a company wants to boost its operating cash flow, it just needs to issue more receivables-backed securities.

For sheer brazenness, few attempts to create the illusion of higher operating cash flows match the games played by WorldCom. The fallen telecom giant is now notorious for violating accounting regulations, and possibly federal law, by treating ordinary expenses as investments, thus grossly distorting both reported earnings and operating cash flow. Contemporaneous reports of the debacle focused on the $3.8 billion boost to net income WorldCom achieved by treating ordinary operating expenses as investments. The same fraudulent accounting decisions also boosted operating cash flow by shifting $3 billion in expenditures from operations to the investment section of the report. While ordinary investors may have been swayed by the profits that WorldCom was able to report, thanks to the fraud, decision makers at large lending institutions may have paid more attention to the cash-flow statement, which, because of the shift, indicated that the company had at least $3 billion more available to service debt than it actually did.

Yes, cash is king, but the cash-flow statement doesn't always present a fair picture of operations. When looking at cash, we recommend that those with a stake in honest financial reporting keep an eye out for murky or unhelpful footnotes and masked or combined transactions that could suggest a more positive cash flow trajectory than is realistic. And for goodness' sake, keep an eye on those options.

Suggestions for Action

If you are an insider, don't allow your business to play the pro forma game. Period.

Outsiders should never use management's pro forma numbers as the basis for conclusions about business performance. Outsiders are encouraged to name their own profit—for using adjustments designed to reveal true performance, not obscure it. If you are consistent with what you include and exclude, you will be able at least to make valid comparisons between years and among competing companies. Other independent alternative earnings measures, such as S&P's core earnings, may add useful and objective insights. As independent measures become more prevalent, they should be considered in developing your own pro forma earnings. Even insiders can find them a source of helpful suggestions about business performance and the accuracy and relevance of the company's financial reports.

As for EBITDA, remember: It is only as reliable as the E that goes into it. In any case, it is only a rough approximation of operating cash flows. If a business only breaks even on EBITDA, it will not generate enough cash to replace basic capital assets used in the business. Insiders and outside parties need to ask: Why does the company prefer EBITDA to conventional earnings? What supposed flaw in conventional earnings is EBITDA supposed to correct? If EBITDA contains adjustments designed to give a clearer picture of tax payments or capital expenditures, how are those adjustments calculated, and are they, in fact, more realistic than the numbers they replace?

When examining cash-flow statements, be sure the cash reported is the kind of cash it purports to be. Each large item in the cash-flow statements should be clearly described. You should be able to easily understand the reasons why each large item is categorized the way it is.

Do operating cash flows vary dramatically from year to year? Does management explain those variations fully and clearly? Does management adequately explain large divergences between earnings and operating cash flow?

In particular, keep an eye on the relationship between the growth in sales and the growth in receivables. Are customers willing and able to pay cash, or is the company boosting sales by extending credit? Such a policy will produce an earnings increase without a proportional increase in operating cash. You will need to make an informed judgment about whether sales today will actually generate cash tomorrow.

Look carefully at the cash-flow-from-operations section of the cash-flow statement. Cash is cash, but not all from operations. Are securities sales, completed at the discretion of management, artificially boosting cash from operations? Are securities purchases creating a reserve to boost future cash from operations when needed? Are there pension transactions that skew cash from operations? Are there financing transactions disguised as operating cash flows? Are there investment transactions, such as customer-acquisition payments for customers that are more accurately described as expenses, and therefore a use of operating cash?

Examine the effect of software development costs reported as investments: How would those costs affect the company's finances if they were treated as expenses, rather than capitalized? Bear in mind that every dollar capitalized has the effect of boosting cash from operations.

10

FAIR VALUE: TOWARD TRUSTWORTHY CORPORATE REPORTING

Most of this book is a chronicle and analysis of deceit and folly, of wrongdoing driven by greed, fueled by arrogance and fear, and sustained by wishful thinking, self-deception, and blind herd instinct. We have attempted to be wide-ranging in our discussion, but we do not claim to be encyclopedic. How could we be? Even as this book was being readied for publication, fresh accounting scandals were breaking out across the globe.

Ahold, the Dutch grocery giant, was facing inquiries over the way it accounted for incentive payments from its suppliers. Reporters and investigators were unraveling a long-running scheme at Health-South Corp. to produce phantom revenue and earnings. And the AOL unit of AOL Time Warner was under renewed scrutiny for inflating revenue—this time, allegedly, by cycling its own money through other companies to make it appear that those companies were buying advertising time on AOL's online service.

The heart sinks before such evidence. It is truly dismaying to see that many corporations, undeterred by the recent scandals, continue to use their financial reports to deceive regulators, investors, their own employees, and the general public. Not only have the leaders of some of America's most prominent corporations shown nothing but disdain for the notions of honesty and fair dealing, they have done so with near-total impunity. And let's be clear. We all pay the price for accounting games, even those of us who don't directly invest in the stock market. When managers render their accounts dishonestly, capital resources are misspent. Instead of capital finding its way to genuine value creators, it migrates to companies and management teams that squander it.

Our concerns were in no way diminished in March 2003, when the New York Stock Exchange nominated to its board—as a representative of the investing public, no less—Citicorp Chairman Sanford Weill. During the boom, Jack Grubman, the star telecom analyst of Citicorp's Salomon Smith Barney unit, enjoyed cozy relationships with World-Com CEO Bernard Ebbers and other telecom executives—he even attended several WorldCom board meetings. Less an analyst than a cheerleader for the companies he covered, Grubman was unabashed about his role. "What was once a conflict," he told *BusinessWeek* in 2000, "is now a synergy." Such comments reveal a casual contempt for the investors who relied on his supposedly objective advice. Simply for continuing to employ Grubman long after his conflicts were exposed, Weill should have been ruled out of contention for the NYSE board post.

But it gets worse: Weill may have urged Grubman in 1999 to raise his rating on AT&T so that Salomon Smith Barney could win a share of AT&T's investment banking business and so that Weill could enlist the aid of AT&T Chairman Michael Armstrong, a Citicorp director, in a boardroom battle. And when Grubman finally resigned in 2002, Citicorp paid him more than $30 million in severance. That NYSE president Richard Grasso would even think of nominating Weill to the NYSE board, especially to advocate the interests of the investing public, says volumes about the investment community's failure to comprehend the severity of the crisis it faces. It also casts serious doubt on the industry's claims that it can police itself.

Given the depth and scope of the crisis in corporate governance and financial reporting, it is easy to be cynical about business's efforts to reform the system from which the crisis emerged—easy, but a mistake. Despite the continued cluelessness exhibited by many business leaders, the public and its elected and appointed representatives have an unprec-edented opportunity here: They can achieve reforms that will significant-ly raise the standard of corporate reporting and strengthen investors' confidence that the profits being reported to them are profits they can trust. But those reforms must be carefully crafted and targeted. Badly conceived and executed reforms will not just retard the reform effort, they may derail it altogether by misdirecting energy and attention to sym-bolic gestures that offer the appearance of reform without the substance.

Too Many Rules, Not Enough Principles?

One of the most widely touted reform initiatives is the attempt to put the leading industrialized nations on a "principles-based" account-ing standard. Many advocates claim that the financial scandals in the United States resulted, at least in part, from the "rules-based" approach of U.S. Generally Accepted Accounting Principles (GAAP). Critics note that U.S. accounting rules in recent years have proliferated to cover seemingly every possible transaction and economic contingency. By their sheer volume, the rules offer clever financial officers, corporate ex-ecutives, and accountants limitless opportunities to "game the sys-tem"—to devise accounting maneuvers that meet the letter of the rules while subverting their intent.

The rules, and business's many successful efforts to skirt them, are seen by critics as evidence of major conceptual and organizational flaws in GAAP. As an alternative they offer International Accounting Standards (IAS), the only legitimate contender with U.S. GAAP for worldwide dominance of corporate financial reporting. By prescribing broad principles that accounting should honor, rather than narrow rules to which it must adhere, IAS would have prevented the United States report-ing scandals from occurring, or at least would have reduced their frequen-cy and the severity of their consequences. Or so IAS's advocates contend.

We believe that there is much value in the critique of U.S. GAAP offered by proponents of IAS. But it does not follow that IAS would have prevented the scandals, much less that it is any sort of panacea. And whatever its flaws, U.S. GAAP provides detailed guidance that is often useful to corporations and investors alike and at times indispens-able. What's more, little will be accomplished by restoring the primacy of principles over detailed rules unless it is accompanied—or perhaps preceded—by important corporate governance reforms.

We will propose a set of reforms later in this chapter. First, though, we will take up the relative merits of rules-based and principles-based accounting. We begin with a bit of history.

The concept of principles-based accounting is hardly unknown in the United States. Until the 1970s, in fact, the accounting standards-setting process in the United States was largely principles based. But almost imperceptibly, the operating philosophy of financial reporting began to change, as capital and commercial market transactions evolved in ways not anticipated in the GAAP established in earlier, simpler times.

Meanwhile, as the philosophy of corporate financial reporting was changing, the business environment in the United States became increasingly litigious. Not only were companies looking for accounting solutions to increasingly complex transactions, they also wanted cover in case they had to defend themselves against shareholder lawsuits. What they wanted, quite simply, was detailed guidance on how to implement GAAP—something that would go beyond basic principles and provide concrete, practical rules for accounting for complex transactions, reliance on which would allow them to prevail in court. Hence the birth of rules-based accounting.

When seen in this way, the advent of rules-based accounting is understandable, even laudable. It arose as a logical response to a serious, recurring business problem. And in the United States, huge intellectual resources—from the big accounting firms and a large cadre of Ph.D.'s at American business schools—could be brought to bear on complex accounting issues.

All this effort and energy, however, produced two unforeseen consequences. First, the complexity of U.S. GAAP increased immensely, mainly because of the exponential increase in the amount of interpretation and implementation guidance provided by the Financial Accounting Standards Board (FASB), the chief guardian and promulgator of GAAP, and other professional bodies such as the American Institute of CPAs. Second, much of the guidance that poured forth from the FASB and elsewhere came at the express request of corporations. When companies intervene in the rulemaking process, it's usually because they want something from it, and what they want may not be in the best interest of investors and the public. Not only are corporations looking for guidance they can point to in the event of litigation, they also seek solutions that promote their own financial reporting objectives.

The result: GAAP is riddled with scores of exceptions to the rules. Exceptions often arise as compromises between the demands of investors and the practical implementation concerns of public accountants and corporate managers. Although some exceptions are relatively harmless from an investor perspective, others are less benign. For example, some exceptions allow companies to avoid a new standard altogether and continue to use the practice in force before it was enacted. Other exceptions allow companies to achieve a desired accounting result, such as keeping a particular debt off-balance-sheet or reducing earnings volatility, which otherwise could not be achieved if the spirit of the standard were fully respected. Such exceptions seem to exist not to promote reliable financial reporting but to protect individual corporations from the adverse consequences that might flow from reliable reporting.

Nowhere is the preponderance of exceptions more obvious than in rules governing derivative instruments and hedging activities. Such matters can be devilishly complex, so it's no surprise that the accounting is complex, too. But compounding the complexity is a myriad of rules, exceptions, and interpretive guidance. The FASB has created a working body, called the Derivatives Implementation Group, to propose solutions to specific practice issues that arise from the implementation of GAAP. As of this writing, the number of such proposals is approaching 200.

Anyone who slogs through the rules, interpretations, exceptions, and exceptions to exceptions that characterize U.S. GAAP welcomes the comparative simplicity and straightforwardness of IAS. IAS is not remotely as detailed or prescriptive as U.S. GAAP, in part because the IASB hasn't been at it as long as the FASB, but also because the IASB's limited budget prevents the sort of detailed investigations that have become the norm in the United States whenever a new standard is proposed. IAS will never have the institutional apparatus to produce the sort of detailed implementation guidance that is all in a day's work at the FASB.

Out of necessity, then, the IASB has adopted a "less-is more" approach that requires companies and their auditors to consider whether the accounting contemplated is consistent with the spirit of a particular underlying principle. Detailed rules on implementation are simply not available. In effect, the IASB's limited funding, long perceived as a curse, has emerged as something of a blessing, at least to anyone attempting to master IAS.

The virtues and attractions of IAS are undeniable, but they do not include the ability to forestall the sort of accounting scandals we have all witnessed recently. Enron and WorldCom did not cleverly exploit loopholes in GAAP, they bypassed the rules altogether. Enron's free fall, for example, began when it was forced to correct its financial statements to bring them in accordance with GAAP. WorldCom's case is even more blatant. Not even the most ingenious or outlandish sophistry could justify the decision by some WorldCom executives to capitalize billions of dollars of what were obviously operating expenses. Both scandals, in other words, came about not because GAAP was being perverted, but because it was being ignored.

Indeed, there is some reason to think that the Enron and World-Com scandals came to light faster in the United States than they would have in a country where IAS governs. In the United States, GAAP is supplemented and supported by a network of formal and informal customs, practices, and conventions that together compel corporations to produce far more information than most other accounting regimes demand. For example, the U.S. Securities and Exchange Commission (SEC)—not U.S. GAAP—requires every annual report to include Management's Discussion and Analysis (MD&A) of financial results. The MD&A can be one of the most valuable elements of an annual report, offering an insider's perspective on company finances, but it is almost unheard-of outside the United States. Likewise, it is the U.S. stock exchanges, not GAAP, that mandate that board members be financially literate. It is the SEC that requires disclosures on how executive compensation is calculated, information not normally available outside the United States. And the Sarbanes-Oxley Act has beefed up the SEC mandate that requires companies to file public reports of significant and unusual corporate events, such as a change of control, the replacement of an audit firm, or the signing of a major contract. Sarbanes-Oxley has expanded the roster of events that must be reported, so that companies must now announce restructurings, changes in debt ratings, and the loss of large customers. Many such events must be reported within five business days. This nearly real-time reporting stands in sharp contrast to reporting regimes in much of the rest of world, where companies disclose their finances only semiannually. We believe that any attempt to adopt principles-based standards, without the U.S. system's additional reporting and governance mandates, would leave the public with less information than it has today.

But there is an even better way to refute those IAS advocates who say: "It couldn't happen here." And that is to reply: "It already has." Financial reporting practices in countries where IAS or other accounting regimes prevail are even worse than in the United States. A recent study of thousands of companies in 31 countries, including the United States, reveals that, on average, earnings management is worse just about everywhere else. Based on several widely accepted measures of accounting manipulation, such as income smoothing, the authors of the study develop an aggregate earnings-management score for each country over the period 1990 to 1999. And which country had the lowest score (implying the least amount of earnings management)? The United States. The Scandinavian countries scored well, as did most of the major English-speaking countries, especially Australia and Canada. Among the worst offenders were Germany, Japan, and Italy, home to some of the most vociferous critics of U.S.-style capitalism and accounting.

The 2003 scandal that engulfed Ahold, the Dutch supermarket giant, is in itself an argument against principles-based accounting. (Ahold prepared its reports according to the Dutch system, which consists of even broader principles than those found in IAS.) Similar scandals will likely follow, as financial transparency finds its way into parts of the world that haven't experienced it yet. It is a statistical certainty that many of the companies falling to scandal will have used principles-based systems, or at least have been certified by their auditors as doing so.

IAS cannot prevent misleading comparisons any more than it can stop corporate managers bent on fraud. The system's broad principles are subject to a wide range of interpretation, not only from one country to another and one firm to another, but even within different offices of the same firm. With so much room for interpretation among practitioners, comparability across companies is routinely compromised. One Big Four accounting firm, concluding that existing interpretations of IAS were too broad and vague, developed a handbook spelling out the firm's official interpretation of the standards. At another Big Four firm, the merger of two client companies sparked a row between the firm's London and Paris offices, which clashed over interpretations of several IAS principles relating to mergers.

We do not raise these issues to discredit IAS or principles-based accounting, but to rein in expectations about what any accounting system, in and of itself, can achieve. Even if the differences between IAS and U.S. GAAP were magically resolved tomorrow and the world's economies adopted a universal accounting regime, the flow of scandal and malfeasance would probably continue unabated. That is because no accounting system can eliminate the need for managerial judgment. No system can predict which customers will and will not pay, how long a building will last, or the future value of a patent or brand. And where there is judgment, there will always be controversy and the potential for manipulation.

To function properly, accounting systems require that managerial judgment be balanced by a countervailing force: professional judgment. But to be a true countervailing force—rather than management's handmaiden, which the accounting profession has become—accounting professionals must reorient their loyalties, placing themselves at the service of shareholders and their representatives, the board of directors. Professional achievement must be measured by the core values of fairness, transparency, and accuracy, not by the financial reporting goals of corporate managers.

The primacy of accurate reporting and sound professional judgment over mere technical compliance with GAAP is more than just a fond wish of the present authors. It has been enshrined in the American legal record. Unlike IAS, U.S. GAAP has been subjected to extensive legal review over the years, and a crucial finding of the courts is that *mere adherence to the letter of the rules is not enough.* In a 1970 case, a U.S. appeals court ruled that "if literal compliance with GAAP creates a fraudulent or materially misleading impression in the minds of shareholders, the accountants could and would be held criminally liable." In other words, criminality flows from the intent to deceive, even if the accountants dot all of GAAP's *i*'s and cross all its *t*'s.

The legal bulwarks that support the U.S. system of financial reporting can be usefully contrasted with those in countries such as the Netherlands, which does not even have an authority empowered to prosecute accounting fraud. We hope, then, that in their haste to adopt the virtues of principles-based accounting, U.S. authorities do not neglect or jettison the virtues of the U.S. system, which is a web of customs, practices, and court rulings, as well as an accounting regime. To the contrary, we hope that sizable elements of the U.S. system are widely adopted elsewhere.

In turn, we hope that the U.S. accounting profession and corporate financial officers reaffirm their allegiance to broad principles. In support of this effort, U.S. rulesmaking bodies should cut away much of the elaborate superstructure of exceptions that has grown up around GAAP. They should hold exceptions to a minimum, allowing them only where practical issues cannot be reasonably solved in some other way. When the FASB provides implementation guidance, its sole purpose should be to help companies and their auditors apply a standard pertaining to a complicated accounting issue in a way that is consistent with the intent and spirit of the standard. Above all, the FASB should put an end to exceptions and guidance that are little more than favors to individual corporations seeking to avoid or soft-pedal unfavorable disclosures or other accounting outcomes.

Severing the Link: How Corporations Must Change

As strongly as we advocate extensive, aggressive accounting reform, however, we do not pretend for a moment that accounting reform alone will ensure the integrity of the financial reporting process. Genuine, comprehensive reform also requires dramatic changes in corporate governance, and more specifically in the way that companies and their boards manage themselves and the audit process. The first step is to adopt the British custom of separating the position of CEO from board chairman, which creates checks and balances unavailable in systems in which the company is run by a single, all-powerful boss. We don't urge adoption of the European system of collective leadership through management boards. We think strong leadership is a blessing—but it does require monitoring and supervision. Such tasks are easier when the board is chaired by someone other than the CEO. A growing number of U.S. companies are moving in this direction, designating lead directors empowered to set the board agenda and chair meetings that discuss sensitive issues in the absence of the CEO and other executive board members.

The next step is just as important: to sever the link between a corporation's management and its outside auditors.

How to reach that end is a matter of great controversy, even among the authors of this book. Some argue that the answer is to require corporations to rotate auditors periodically – every five years is an oft-repeated suggestion. Those in favor of such a move point to Arthur Andersen's notorious handling of Waste Management (WM), the scandal-plagued garbage hauler. From 1992 until 1998, WM overstated earnings by $1.7 billion, largely by improperly deferring or understating expenses and manipulating reserve accounts. Arthur Andersen detected the phony accounting, but instead of requiring WM to restate immediately, the accounting firm allowed WM to make corrections over a ten-year period. Had Arthur Andersen not been so eager to preserve a long-term relationship with its client, say advocates of the five-year rotation, it would have done the right thing and demanded an immediate restatement rather than let the infractions slide.

Opponents of this view—including one of this book's co-authors—counter that mandating the rotation of audit firms might actually reduce the quality of audits. If audit firms are rotated every five years, what will become of the knowledge of a company's culture and practices that accumulates over the course of a long-term audit engagement? Rather than rotate audit firms, says this school of thought, rotate the audit *partners* (as is now required in the United States under the recent Sarbanes-Oxley bill). Given the way that partner compensation is managed at most large accounting firms, high-profile clients translate into high personal income for the auditors in charge. If the amount of personal income that any one partner can expect from a single client is limited by a five-year mandate, partners will face less temptation to indulge in such nudge-and-wink deals as that between Andersen and WM.

That debate will not be settled here, and in any case it is a secondary consideration. A sure way to sever the link between management and auditors is to have both internal and external audit staffs report to the board of directors—and specifically the audit committee—rather than to the CEO or CFO. Likewise, the board, not management, should pay the outside audit firm.

The head of the audit committee, who like all committee members should be independent of the corporation, must consciously cultivate a close relationship with the audit partner and must also possess a healthy degree of skepticism and assertiveness. Regular consultations are a must. Where practical, a member of the audit committee should be present at key meetings of management and members of either the internal or external audit team. The point of all these changes is to compel auditors to view investors, and their proxy the audit committee, as the true client.

A priority for audit committees at global corporations is to assess auditor competence in all the countries where the company does business. We might have a high degree of confidence when we're told that the reports of a Danish or Norwegian firm are prepared in accordance with IAS, but what is such an assurance worth for a Singaporean or Malaysian business? Auditors around the world tend to be as influenced by local culture as by international norms. For instance, Japanese audits are often ineffectual because of that nation's strong cultural bias against challenging authority figures.

Besides, some overseas auditors are simply incompetent. BDO International, a second-tier firm, was humiliated in 2003 by the revelation that one of its clients, ACLN Ltd. of Cyprus, had created an entirely fictitious line of business. ACLN claimed to be exporting used cars from Europe to Africa and selling new cars in Africa, and it faked documentation to that effect. Rather than independently verifying bank balances or customers, the accounting firm took ACLN's word for it. BDO's negligence was revealed following ACLN's inevitable collapse; the firm settled the matter by forfeiting its audit fee.

Such horror stories point up the need for audit-committee awareness of accounting practices everywhere the company does business. If a particular country contributes a large share of revenue, profits, or assets, the audit partner for that country should be interviewed and scrutinized by the audit committee as if he or she were the lead partner. The committee should not be afraid to replace auditors in other countries or even parachute in auditors from the United States, Canada, or the United Kingdom.

Corporate boards must also take ownership of key governance and reporting processes. In particular, boards must oversee management's discussion of critical accounting policies (CAPs) and executive compensation. We'll take up the matter of CAPs first. The Sarbanes-Oxley Act of 2002 requires management to publicly discuss and defend its CAPs as part of the Management Discussion and Analysis. Of course, companies have had to discuss major accounting choices in the past, conventionally in the first footnote to the financial statements. But such notes tend to be cryptic and not especially helpful. Sarbanes-Oxley is likely to prompt a more intelligible discussion, although the proof will be in the practice. At present, the role of the board in the preparation and review of the Management Discussion and Analysis has not been formalized. We recommend that the audit committee review and approve the CAP disclosures as well as the entire MD&A. And we believe that management's CAPs disclosure should:

1. Describe the impact of different accounting choices on earnings.
2. Specify the policies that are considered *non*critical and defend its judgment in this regard. Matters such as foreign exchange, taxes, derivatives, and pensions are almost always critical. Management should have to defend any choice to deem them otherwise.
3. Explicitly discuss the current and future earnings impact of changes in interest rates, exchange rates, commodity prices, and other key variables.

In addition, the auditors should comment on all material changes in accounting policies. Such a requirement would force to the surface any new or unorthodox accounting choices and allow directors and the public to evaluate their appropriateness.

We also encourage audit committees to consider expanded reporting on nonfinancial and forward-looking measures. We recognize that while a company's own assessment of innovation in the laboratory, customer satisfaction, human resource development, and the like, is inherently subjective, such things are known to drive shareholder value. Valuation controversies will arise, to be sure, but a number of firms specializing in intangibles valuation have recently sprung up. And with recent changes in goodwill accounting that now compel businesses to identify a broader range of intangibles in the companies they acquire, accountants and other professionals will certainly gain more expertise in this area over the coming years. As they gain such expertise, they can then help boards make informed assessments and deliver reports on nonfinancial indicators that are informative and useful without giving away the store. Some companies, such as Monsanto, are beginning to report on such matters. The company's Web site features a discussion of the new products in its pipeline and their stage of development. We look forward to the day when the disclosure of such information becomes as routine as the financial measures companies have produced for generations.

Updates on intangibles will not eliminate deceptive reporting, however. Companies that issue misleading earnings reports are also likely to issue misleading reports on new product initiatives, new lines of business, and expansion into new markets. And comparisons of such reports with prior years and with similar reports by competitors will create a whole new class of benchmarking headaches.

Like the audit committee, the compensation committee should consist of directors who are not employees of the corporation. At least one member of the comp committee should be financially literate; ideally, the audit committee and the comp committee would have at least one member in common. A thorough grounding in financial-reporting issues is essential to the comp committee's function, if only because many if not most compensation decisions are based on financial targets, particularly profit and revenue targets. Financially literate comp-committee members will also have a duty to assess and challenge the compensation consultants advising the board on executive pay. Such consultants will be much less likely to propose misleading benchmarks if they know their every move is being scrutinized by a savvy and independent director.

Financial literacy, we should point out here, is not merely a matter of MBAs, accounting degrees, and other academic credentials. True financial literacy is as much art as science and involves an understanding of human nature as well as debits and credits. It is acquired only through experience with both business and the world. A handful of generally smaller accounting firms have seized upon the expanding need for financial literacy to open a new line of business, offering their accounting and financial expertise on a consulting basis to board members and especially audit committees. Provided that such firms have experience in the sort of accounting issues that arise in large public corporations, their advice can offer a useful way to reality-test management's assertions and offer second opinions on major accounting questions.

Any discussion of executive compensation inevitably raises the issue of stock options. Our opinion on this matter is straightforward. They should be expensed. And please, spare us the argument about the weaknesses of Black-Scholes and other valuation models. Nothing is more disingenuous than managers who grant themselves stock options, knowing quite well that they have value, and who then complain that options should not be expensed because they can't be valued with precision. Yes, IAS and U.S. GAAP now disagree about valuation and about smaller questions, such as how to treat options that never vest. But we expect these differences to be harmonized in fairly short order. In the meantime, let's call a halt to the debate: Options are an expense and should be treated as such.

The Agenda for the Rest of Us:
Call Off the Earnings Game

We do not want to leave the impression that corporations and audit firms alone must change. True financial reform also demands the participation of analysts, journalists, shareholders, and the public at large. By looking at the stock market as a sporting contest and quarterly earnings as the means of keeping score, journalists, analysts, and shareholders have been complicit in the accounting games of recent years. They have all but invited management to "make their number"—reach the quarterly earnings target—by almost any means necessary. That's why companies rarely miss their number by small margins. A company would never report earnings of 87 cents per share if its quarterly EPS target were 88 cents. That would set off too many alarm bells. After all, couldn't the company have recovered hidden reserves, or stuffed the channel, or done *something* to scrape up that extra one cent? As a stockbroker once told one of the authors, "Things must be pretty bad if they can't come up with one lousy penny." By playing along so enthusiastically with the earnings game, analysts, journalists, and investors deserve a fair amount of the blame for the sad state of corporate financial reporting. They'll get better accounting when they insist on it.

To some extent, we are encouraged by the massive coverage that the financial press has lavished on suspicious accounting since the Enron meltdown. For the moment, anyway, journalists recognize the importance of honest financial reporting to the proper functioning of the world's capital markets. We just hope it's not a fad.

We do not have a solution for the human susceptibility to fads—if nothing else, the recent boom and bust prove that analysts, journalists, and investors are human, too. We only have a plea for common sense, skepticism, and restraint. During the dot-com boom, many reporters were little more than cheerleaders for the companies they covered. The same goes for analysts, especially those who did the bidding of the investment-banking side of their firms. To make amends for their lack of vigilance—or worse—we believe that both the news media and the financial-services industry have an obligation to invest in financial-literacy education, both for their own employees and for the public at large. Analysts and journalists must once again become an effective force for uncovering and publicizing untrustworthy profit reports and other questionable corporate assertions.

Like analysts and reporters, shareholders must also recognize that there are no shortcuts to successful investing. Now that the bubble has burst, hot tips and momentum won't cut it. Investors must make the effort to inform themselves. In practical terms, that means they have to demand the corporate data they need to make an informed judgment, rather than wait for the data to come to them. Did you know that most states, as a matter of law, grant inspection rights to shareholders? These rights give shareholders the right to inspect crucial corporate information that many companies would rather keep quiet. One shareholder of TLC Beatrice International, incorporated in Delaware, exercised his right to inspect the company's related-party transactions. The inspection revealed a highly questionable deal that prompted a civil complaint, which TLC Beatrice settled before trial. Most U.S. companies are incorporated in Delaware, where by law a shareholder can assert a right to inspection by presenting a notarized letter identifying specific documents to be inspected. If an answer to a legitimate request is not forthcoming from the corporation within five days, the Delaware chancery court will enforce the request with an order. Details on investor inspection rights in other states can be requested from the secretary of state.

Even without mobs of shareholders exercising their inspection rights, corporations and their managers feel themselves under increased scrutiny these days. Everyone is watching more closely. Auditors are asking more questions, and they're being answered with more care and not a little anxiety. As evidenced by a steady rise in audit fees, audits are reaching wider and digging deeper, with management's encouragement—a welcome consequence of the Sarbanes-Oxley Act's requirement that the CEO and CFO of every company sign off on the company's financial reports.

At the same time, the weakening economy has moderated growth expectations, easing the competitive pressure to puff up sales and earnings. But the climate is sure to change eventually. When economic activity accelerates and the stock market heads north again, the temptation to cheat will grow stronger, and it will become more difficult to remember the lessons of the past. New transactions and business models will continue to emerge, and accounting systems will have to adapt.

More to the point, so will we. For the survival of our economic system, we will have to stop treating deceptive financial reporting as an offense that harms no one and begin to see it as an offense against us all. Few of the executives who cooked their books during the boom will end up going to jail—most of the criminal convictions arising from the bursting of the bubble will be for such offenses as insider trading, embezzlement, and tax evasion. That is probably as it should be. Ultimately, the damage that deceptive financial reporting does is social. The penalty should be social as well. We do not believe in mandatory firing for CEOs whose companies are forced to restate—circumstances alter cases, after all. But we will applaud when a board sacks a CEO who has embarrassed his company and hurt his shareholders by fudging the numbers, and we will applaud more loudly when he is stripped of his severance pay and benefits—and stock options. We will applaud still more loudly when such a CEO resigns without prompting. At that point, we will be confident that society sees dishonest financial reporting for what it is—a disgrace.

Ultimately, what is so surprising—and disappointing—about the outrage over the postboom financial scandals is that it is not greater and more widespread. The catastrophes of Enron, WorldCom, Adelphia, HealthSouth, and the rest came only a few years after NASDAQ's $1 billion settlement for colluding to inflate trading costs for investors. That scandal, in turn, followed hard on the heels of the insider-trading, junk-bond, and savings-and-loan scandals of the 1980s. This widespread, large-scale, serial corporate corruption does tremendous violence to the social fabric, fraying the assumption of good faith that's a prerequisite for a functioning market. Since September 11, 2001, the United States and the other industrialized democracies have—with good reason—been preoccupied with shadowy external threats. It would be a terrible irony if the greatest threat to capitalism turned out to be the capitalists.

INDEX

8 reasons why you should read the Financial Times for 4 weeks RISK-FREE!

To help you stay current with significant
developments in the world economy ...
and to assist you to make informed business
decisions — the Financial Times brings you:

❶ Fast, meaningful overviews of international affairs ... plus daily briefings on major world news.

❷ Perceptive coverage of economic, business, financial and political developments with special focus on emerging markets.

❸ More international business news than any other publication.

❹ Sophisticated financial analysis and commentary on world market activity plus stock quotes from over 30 countries.

❺ Reports on international companies and a section on global investing.

❻ Specialized pages on management, marketing, advertising and technological innovations from all parts of the world.

❼ Highly valued single-topic special reports (over 200 annually) on countries, industries, investment opportunities, technology and more.

❽ The Saturday Weekend FT section — a globetrotter's guide to leisure-time activities around the world: the arts, fine dining, travel, sports and more.

FT FINANCIAL TIMES
World business newspaper

The *Financial Times* delivers a world of business news.

Use the Risk-Free Trial Voucher below!

To stay ahead in today's business world you need to be well-informed on a daily basis. And not just on the national level. You need a news source that closely monitors the entire world of business, and then delivers it in a concise, quick-read format.

With the *Financial Times* you get the major stories from every region of the world. Reports found nowhere else. You get business, management, politics, economics, technology and more.

Now you can try the *Financial Times* for 4 weeks, absolutely risk free. And better yet, if you wish to continue receiving the *Financial Times* you'll get great savings off the regular subscription rate. Just use the voucher below.

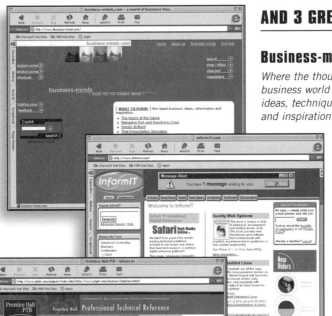